Pennsylvania's Rail-Trails

7th Edition

Tom Sexton • Jamie Bridges

RAILS
- to -
TRAILS
CONSERVANCY

Northeast Regional Office

Published by Rails-to-Trails Conservancy
Northeast Regional Office
Harrisburg, PA 17101
717-238-1717

ISBN 0-925794-17-1

Acknowledgments

The 7th edition of *Pennsylvania's Rail-Trails* is a continuation of facts gathered by many individuals over several years. Craig Warner, Steve Spindler, Fran Buffington, Julie Larson, Bill Metzger and Pam Metzger added much to earlier editions.

While too numerous to list, a heart-felt thanks to the rail-trail volunteers who provided historical background, cartographic materials, and select photographs. The trail volunteers are by far the #1 reason Pennsylvania is home to so many rail-trails.

And lastly, thanks to the many trailside bike shops, outfitters, restaurants, coffee houses, bed and breakfasts, and campgrounds who support *Pennsylvania's Rail-Trails* as trailside business partners.

Introduction

Imagine a network of trails across America connecting our cities, towns and countrysides. Locally this network will link our neighborhoods with our schools, workplaces, shopping areas, and parks, helping to serve community transportation needs as well as meet the growing demand for close to home recreation.

In Pennsylvania, with the dedication in June 2001 of our 1000th mile of rail-trail on the Lebanon Valley Rail-Trail, the dream may not be so far-fetched. This guidebook contains information on over 1100 miles of rail-trail. With our tremendous rail-trail growth rate, this guidebook is very much a "living document" which requires updates on an annual basis.

In addition to leading the nation in open rail-trails and rail-trails under development, the Keystone State will serve as a linchpin for a system of interstate rail-trails much as it did for a network of interstate railroads.

We share the first interstate rail-trail — the 12-mile Stavich Trail, which opened in 1983, stretches west from New Castle to Struthers, Ohio. In 1999 the Heritage Rail-Trail County Park in York opened a 21-mile southern connection which stretches into Maryland where an additional 20 miles of trail connects almost to Baltimore.

Pennsylvania's 100th open rail-trail, the Panhandle Trail in Washington County, continues towards completion and will soon connect to Weirton, West Virginia for a total of 29 miles. Also, 100 miles of the Great Allegheny Passage, from McKeesport to Meyersdale, are open. This contiguous rail-trail includes seven different trails and will soon stretch south across the Maryland border and link with the C & O Canal Towpath — and then to Washington, DC for a total of 300 miles!

In Philadelphia, planning for the Delaware River Heritage Trail is moving forward. This 50-mile loop in Pennsylvania and New Jersey utilizes much of the old Kensington & Tacony line.

Near the Delaware Water Gap, the Brodhead Greenway could connect with New Jersey's 27-mile Paulinskill Trail across the Delaware River via the 800-foot pedestrian bridge in Portland.

On the New York border, the remainder of the Delaware & Hudson corridor has been purchased and now extends north from Carbondale 39 miles to the state line. And on Lake Erie, county planners and the Presque Isle Cycling Club are working to purchase five miles of abandoned rail line from Corry into Chautauqua County, New York that connects with two open rail-trails.

I haven't mentioned all the projects, but as you can see Pennsylvania is the key to creating a network of rail-trails across America.

Tom Sexton, Director
Rails-to-Trails Conservancy
Northeast Regional Office

How to Use this Guide

The map on pages 2 and 3 shows the general location of rail-trails in Pennsylvania. The rail-trails are listed in alphabetical order.

Individual trail maps and details about each rail-trail can be found beginning on page 4. Along with a history of the rail-trail and its highlights, we have included specific information about endpoints, mileage, surfaces and permitted uses.

Trailside business partners are listed on the trail maps, and again in the alphabetical appendix on page 164. Please utilize the listings as these partners possess expert knowledge of the trail as well as the locale. Whenever possible, please thank partners for supporting the rail-trail movement in Pennsylvania.

Beneath each trail map, beside the page number, is a map of Pennsylvania that depicts where the trail is located in Pennsylvania.

In addition, we have provided the name of a local contact or agency for you to contact for more information about each rail–trail. Many of the local contacts have detailed maps and brochures. On some of the trails, we have also listed the local contact's e-mail and or website addresses. If the trail is shown as under development, the local contact will be able to give you more information about when the trail will be completed.

Please be mindful of your own safety. Wear a bike helmet, and make sure your family and friends do the same. And have fun!

Activities and Services in this Guide

 walking, running, hiking

 cross-country skiing

 horseback riding

 bicycling

 mountain biking recommended

 inline skating permitted

 snowmobiling

 all-terrain vehicle access

 canoe access

 fishing access

 wheelchair access

 parking area

 bike shop

 food

 bed and breakfast

campground

Key to Trails

——— rail-trail

— — — under development

——— connecting trail

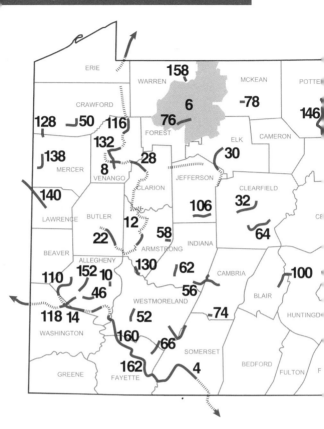

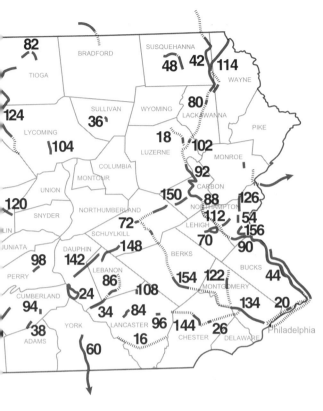

Allegheny Highlands Trail

The Western Maryland Railroad Connellsville Extension, opened in 1912, was a latecomer to the railroad scene. It was part of the "Alphabet Route," an important through-freight route between Chicago and New York, but was abandoned in 1975.

Destined to be a major component of the trail from Pittsburgh to Washington, DC, the Allegheny Highlands Trail follows the Casselman River at an easy grade through the rugged Allegheny Plateau, allowing bicyclists and hikers to travel through the numerous ridges, not over them.

The trail features many reminders of the railroad's past — most notably the freshly resurfaced Salisbury Viaduct, shown above. Mt. Davis, the state's highest point at 3,213 feet, stands just south of the trail. The trail also passes Fort Hill, an ancient Algonquin encampment excavated by archeologists in 1939.

To access the trail at Rockwood, take the PA Turnpike to Exit 110 to 601 south towards Somerset. Continue approximately five blocks, passing the Somerset County Courthouse — the highest courthouse in Pennsylvania. Turn right on W. Main Street, and then turn left on Edgewood Avenue. Edgewood Avenue becomes Water Level Road. Follow Water Level Road nine miles through Rockwood. Turn left on Bridge Street, crossing the CSX tracks and the Casselman River to trailhead parking.

Note: the section between Meyersdale Station and the Salisbury Viaduct is scheduled to be improved during 2002.

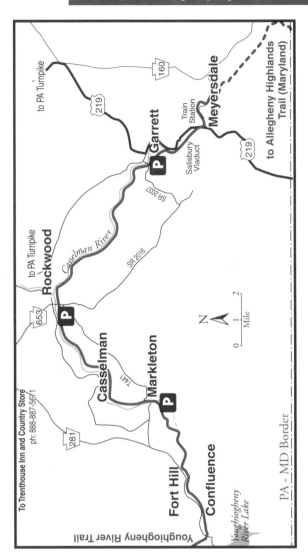

Location:	Somerset County
Miles:	21
Endpoints:	Fort Hill to Meyersdale
Surface:	Crushed limestone

Hank Parke
Somerset County Rails-to-Trails Assoc.
PO Box 413
Somerset, PA 15501
814-445-6431
www.atatrail.org

Allegheny National Forest Trails

Encompassing half a million acres, the Allegheny National Forest is criss-crossed with numerous hiking trails that take advantage of the many old logging roads, abandoned railroad grades, and utility rights-of-way within the forest. Portions of these trails use abandoned railroad grades. These trails are rugged and narrow. They are listed together for that reason. Most of them follow portions of the Tionesta Valley Railroad, a logging railroad abandoned since 1939.

1. Brush Hollow XC Ski Trail (6.9 miles) is blazed with blue diamonds. Skiers with a wide range of expertise will find a challenging experience.

2. Heart's Content XC Ski Trail (6.4 miles) is blazed with blue diamonds. The trail loops around stands of ancient beech, hemlock, and white pine.

3. Kelletville to Nebraska Trace (12.2 miles) follows the long abandoned Sheffield and Tionesta Railroad Grade, which was constructed in the 1880's for lumbering, freight and occasional passenger use. See page 72 for a complete listing.

4. Little Drummer Historical Pathway (3.1 miles) is located in the Owl's Nest area. The trail traverses a designated Watchable Wildlife Area. The Little Drummer Historical Pathway accommodates foot-travel only.

5. Marienville ATV/Bike Trail (36.8 miles) is blazed with yellow diamonds. The trail is divided into Bike Trail and ATV Trail with differing terrain between trails.

6. Mill Creek Trail (5.6 miles) is blazed with white diamonds. Traversing gently rolling terrain, the trail connects Brush Hollow Trail with Twin Lakes Trail.

7. Minister Creek Trail (6.6 miles) is blazed with white diamonds. The trail passes several campsites along Minister Creek and connects with the North Country Scenic Trail.

8. North Country National Scenic Trail (86.4 miles) is blazed with blue diamonds. Part of a 3,200-mile National Scenic Trail, the North Country Trail travels past waterfalls, historic areas, and old hardwood stands. The North Country Trail accommodates foot-travel only.

9. Rocky Gap ATV/Bike Trail (20.8 miles) is blazed with yellow diamonds. The trail is used by ATV and motorbikes.

10. Tidioute Riverside RecTrek Trail (4.5 miles) follows the Allegheny River, and boasts a waterfall, a valley of ferns and a variety of wildflowers, birds and animals.

11. Twin Lakes Trail (15.8 miles) is blaved with white diamonds. The trail connects the North Country Scenic Trail with Twin Lakes Recreation Area.

12. Hickory Creek Trail (11 miles) loops about low-lying wilderness area dominated by lush forest scenes of diverse flora and fauna.

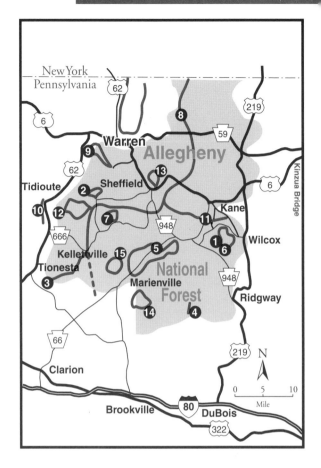

13. Deer Lick Cross Country Ski Trail (9 miles) Traverses creek bed landscape near the small town of Sheffield off historic Route 6.

14. Loleta Trail (3 miles) Follows scenic Millstone Creek, traversing a segment of turn-of-the-century rail line.

15. Beaver Meadows Trail (5.5 miles) Meanders from campground around a lake that feeds Salmon Creek.

Contact: USDA Forest Service,
Allegheny National Forest
222 Liberty Street
Warren, PA 16365-2304
814-723-5150
814-726-2710 (TTY)
www.penn.com/~anf

Allegheny River Trail

The Allegheny River Trail extends south from the Samuel Justus Recreational Trail in Franklin, and stretches to Brandon on the abandoned Allegheny Valley Line. The trail follows a segment of the Allegheny River included in the National Wild and Scenic Rivers System.

After its abandonment in 1984, the line was acquired by the Scrubgrass Generating Company and donated to the non-profit Allegheny Valley Trails Association. This group is building an extensive rail-trail system in northwestern Pennsylvania and hopes to make this trail a part of a bigger network from the Great Lakes to the nation's capitol.

About five miles down the river from Franklin is the Belmar railroad bridge (built in 1907), which offers a spectacular view of the river and connects with the new Sandy Creek Trail. Currently the Sandy Creek Trail runs east to the Village of Van, but will soon connect with the Clarion Highlands Trail.

Nine miles further, Indian God Rock can be found along the trail. These Native American rock carvings date from 1200-1750 and are listed in the National Register of Historic Places.

To access the Allegheny River Trail in Franklin, take PA8 north to its juncture with US322. Take US322 as it becomes 8th Street and crosses the Allegheny River. Trailhead parking is on the right after the bridge. The lot is signed for the Samuel Justus Trail, which is the trail north from Franklin.

To access both the Allegheny River and Sandy Creek Trails in Belmar, take PA8 south from Franklin three miles. Turn left on Pone Lane and pass Franklin High School to Belmar Road. Turn right on Belmar and follow the road to trailhead parking at the river.

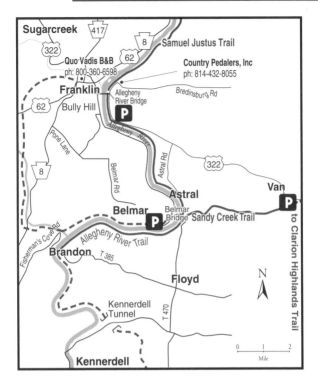

Location:	Venango County
Miles:	10
Endpoints:	Franklin to Brandon
Surface:	Asphalt
Contact:	David Howes
	Allegheny Valley Trails Association
	153 Sixth Avenue
	Clarion, PA 16214
	814-226-6455
	Email: avta@clarion.edu
	Web: http://avta-trails.org

Arboretum Trail

From 1853 to 1856, the Allegheny Valley Railroad was built from Pittsburgh to Kittanning, passing right through the heart of Oakmont Borough. In 1903, Oakmont's rail service improved greatly when the Pennsylvania Railroad opened its Brilliant Cutoff, linking the AVR with other sections of the City.

Declining rail traffic in the 1960s led Conrail to close one of the two tracks in the Borough and during the 1970s the inactive track was removed. In 1995, the corridor was sold —back to the Allegheny Valley Railroad!

A shining example of what dedicated volunteers can accomplish, the Arboretum Trail is also one of Pennsylvania's nine rail-with-trails, where trains and trail users share a corridor. Conceived by the Garden Club of Oakmont in 1989 as a centennial gift to the community, the Arboretum Trail is a part of Oakmont's Boulevard Project, an ambitious plan for the renovation of a downtown business corridor.

The Garden Club raised $3 million for trail construction, landscaping and renovation to the corridor's surroundings, and long-term maintenance of the plantings installed along the Boulevard. An oasis of green and growing beauty and a tangible asset to its community, the Arboretum Trail is a delight in all seasons.

From the Pennsylvania Turnpike, take Exit 48 (Allegheny Valley) and bear right past the toll booth. Follow the signs to Oakmont and cross the Hulton Bridge approximately one mile from the exit. Turn right just before or just after the railroad crossing on Hulton Road, onto either Allegheny Avenue or Allegheny River Boulevard, to find a parking space. The trail lies between the two streets. From downtown Pittsburgh, take Route 28 north to the Blawnox Exit. Continue straight along Route 28 to the Hulton Bridge on the right. Remember, this is a walking trail only.

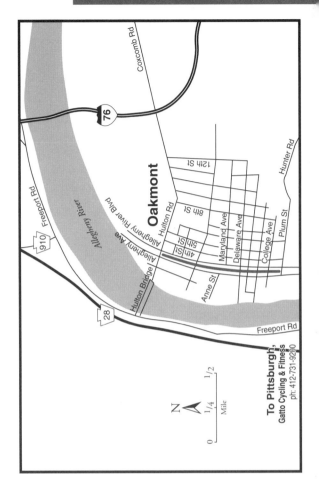

Location: Allegheny County
Miles: 1
Endpoints: Oakmont Borough
Surface: Asphalt
Contact: Kitty Vagley
                 Oakmont Garden Club
                 769 Fifth Street
                 Oakmont, PA 15139
                 412-826-9295

Armstrong Trail

Begun in 1853, the Allegheny Valley Railroad reached Brady's Bend in 1867. Originally built to haul coal, it also became an important oil route after petroleum was discovered further north. Fortunately, the Armstrong County Conservancy began spearheading an effort to preserve the right-of-way a year earlier and provided funds to start the Allegheny Valley Land Trust. The Trust then secured a quarter million dollar loan to purchase the line from Conrail.

Beginning at Schenley (the former site of the Schenley Distillery), the Armstrong Trail passes by many Industrial Age remnants. The trail also features the Brady's Bend tunnel, built in 1915 to bypass a loop in the river, thus shortening the line by about five miles.

The trail surface in Ford City (1.4 miles) is asphalt. The one mile section between Kittanning and Manorville is surfaced with crushed limestone. A 2.3 mile section of asphalt trail is scheduled for construction in Kittanning Borough during 2002. A 1.5 mile section of crushed limestone trail between Kittanning and the mouth of Cowanshannock Creek is scheduled for construction also in 2002. Both projects will be funded with Enhancement dollars. Other sections of the trail are unimproved with varying surface conditions.

Parking is available in several locations along the 52.5-mile corridor. The Kittaning trailhead is the easiest to access. From Pittsburgh and points south, travel Rt28 to the intersection of Rt28, Rt66, and Rt422. At the bottom of the Indiana Pike, park in the Park-n-Ride lot and enter the trail via the handicap access ramp.

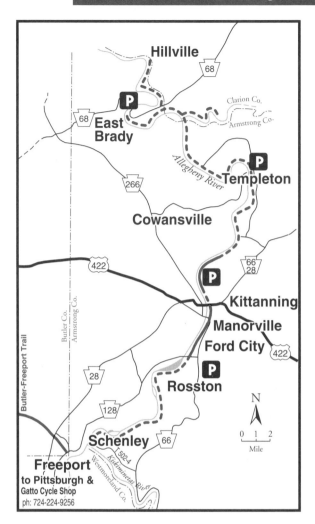

Location: Armstrong and Clarion Counties
Miles: 52.5, 2.4 improved
Endpoints: Schenley to Upper Hillville
Surface: Unimproved surface, 1.4 miles asphalt/
1.0 mile crushed limestone
Contact: Allegheny Valley Land Trust
Kittanning Visitors Center
Market and Water Sts.
PO Box 777
Kittanning, PA 16201
724-543-4478
www.trfn.clpgh.org/avlt/

13

Arrowhead Trail

Originally, the Montour Railroad carried coal to local coke ovens and provided connections to the Ohio River. It was purchased in 1975 by the Pittsburgh & Lake Erie Railroad (P&LE) and abandoned in 1980. Peters Township then purchased the right-of-way and 100 acres to create the Arrowhead Trail, which opened in 1985.

The Arrowhead Trail received the Excellence in Highway Design Award in a statewide competition conducted by the Pennsylvania Department of Transportation. It's not hard to figure out why the trail won the honor; the township has planted 500 trees along the trail.

On a trip along the Arrowhead Trail, you'll travel by wooded and suburban areas and pass through Peterswood Park. The asphalt surface is great for bicycling or in-line skating, and is accessible for individuals with disabilities.

During 2002, the oldest section of the trail will be widened and resurfaced. And the Bethel Spur should be completed also.

From Pittsburgh, head south on Route 19 to Donaldson Crossroads. At Donaldson Crossroads, head left on East McMurray Road. Stay on East McMurray for three miles and head right at the four-way intersection on Valley Brook Road. Continue on Valley Brook one mile to T intersection with Bebout Road. Head right, under the tunnel, and continue 200 yards to Peterswood Park and park. Access the trail at Shelter #4.

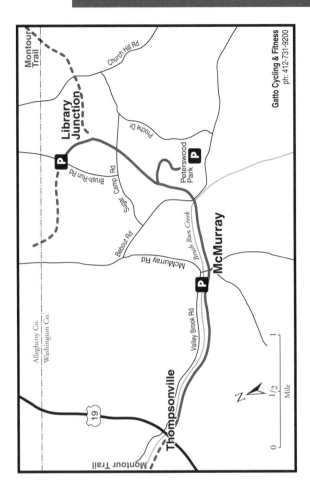

 on certain sections

Location:	Washington County
Miles:	4
Endpoints:	Thompsonville to Library Junction
Surface:	Mostly asphalt, original ballast
Contact:	Ed Fegas
	Peters Township Parks & Recreation Dept.
	610 East McMurray Road
	McMurray, PA 15317
	724-942-5000

Atglen-Susquehanna Trail

The Pennsylvania Railroad's Atglen-Susquehanna Line (also known as the Low Grade Line) was an engineering marvel. Despite the hilly terrain of southern Lancaster County, the line boasted no grade steeper than 1% and no curve greater than two degrees. Built as a freight line to bypass the Main Line passenger service to Philadelphia, construction commenced in 1902 with an estimated cost of $19.5 million. Historic stone bridges, brick-lined tunnels and the 600-foot long, 130-foot high Martic Forge Trestle are a few of the structures whose construction required the talents of laborers of many cultures and nationalities.

We hope the vision of turning this 23-mile railroad line into a rail-trail survives the buffeting winds of local politics. The Friends of the Atglen-Susquehanna Trail refuse to give up their dream. Preservation of the corridor — of which construction claimed the lives of 200 workers — is believed by FAST and many supporting organizations and individuals in Lancaster County to be a vital part of the County's Open Space Plan.

And what a trail it will make!

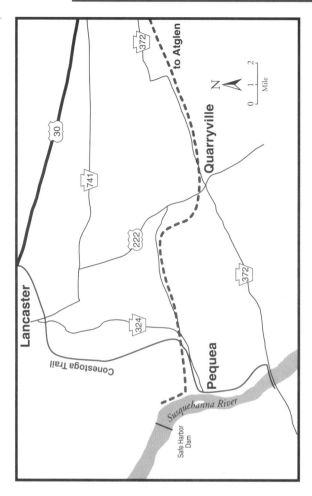

Location:	Lancaster County
Miles:	23
Endpoints:	Atglen to the Susquehanna River to Safe Harbor
Surface:	Undeveloped
Contact:	Julie Nettke
	Friends of the Atglen-Susquehanna Trail, Inc.
	PO Box 146
	Quarryville, PA 17560
	717-786-9055

Back Mountain Trail

The Back Mountain Trail, originally built by lumber and ice king Albert Lewis of Wyoming Valley 115 years ago, was acquired by Lehigh Valley RR in 1887. Lumber, ice, leather goods and anthracite coal were milled, tanned, mined and routed to Urban Markets and Steel Mills from the Endless Mountains and Susquehanna River Basin well into the 1940s.

LVRR was abandoned in 1963. In 1996, Anthracite Scenic Trails Association acquired easements and recorded deeds with Luzerne County for public use of the corridor. Eventually, 15 miles will be developed from Riverfront Park on the Susquehanna River in Wilkes-Barre to Harvey's Lake, bringing back past memories and beginning a new mode of travel in the region.

Diversity abounds in the first two miles, including a waterfall, secluded shady stretches, far reaching views well above the highway, and meadows with flowers. Scarlet tanagers, turkeys, and hawks have been observed, and trout are caught in Toby's Creek. Shops, cafes, and restaurants offer a variety of choices on Main Street in Luzerne.

To reach the Back Mountain Trail, take SR 309, Cross Valley Highway, to Exit 5 (Luzerne). Look for BMT logo directional signs on light poles. Turn right on Union Street at the Exit light. Turn right at the next light into downtown Luzerne. Turn left at the stop sign onto Main Street and proceed along Main Street for two blocks. Go straight at the four way stop sign onto Parry Street. Do not cross over the bridge. The Luzerne trailhead begins where Parry Street turns at a right angle. Parking is available a short distance before the Luzerne trailhead at the Knights of Columbus parking lot (use gravel area). Walk up sidewalk or ride bike to trailhead.

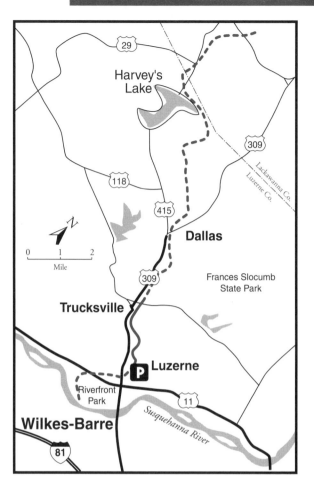

Location:	Luzerne County
Miles:	2.2
Endpoints:	Parry Street in Luzerne to Carver Road in Trucksville
Surface:	Crushed Limestone
Contact:	Anthracite Scenic Trails Association
	PO Box 212
	Dallas, PA 18612
	570-675-9016

Bristol Spurline Park

In 1834, the Philadelphia and Trenton Railroad came to Bristol, a bustling little port where the Delaware Division of the Pennsylvania canal system met the tidewater of the Delaware River.

The canal still exists in Bristol, but the original main line of the Philadelphia and Trenton was relocated in 1882 and it became an industrial spur. The relocated line is now Amtrak's New York to Washington main line, one of the most heavily traveled passenger railroads in the country.

Conrail donated the line to the town of Bristol and the trail was opened in 1980.

Traversing downtown Bristol, this residential trail will eventually connect with the canal at Bath Road and with the Delaware River near Green Lane Road. This asphalt-surfaced trail also connects with nearby playing fields, parks, the elementary school and retirement communities.

Take the Pennsylvania Turnpike to Bristol exit. Take Green Lane into Borough of Bristol. Then follow Radcliffe Street to Mill Street. The trailhead is ahead on the right; the trail runs parallel to the street.

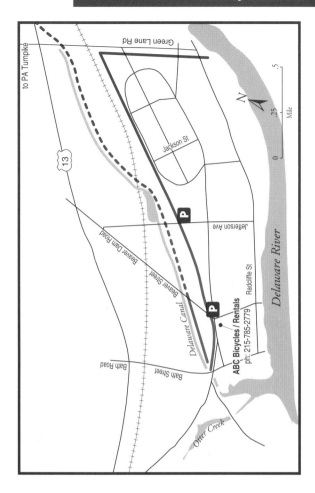

Location: Bucks County
Miles: 2.5
Endpoints: Mill Street to Radcliffe Street, Bristol
Surface: Asphalt
Contact: Borough of Bristol
250 Pond Street
Bristol, PA 19007
215-788-3828

Butler-Freeport Community Trail

In 1871, the first railroad in Butler County started operations. After a two-day celebration for the railroad's opening, a mock funeral was held for the stagecoach that ran between Butler and Freeport.

Built as a branch of the Western Pennsylvania Railroad, the Butler line tapped the high quality limestone deposits vital to Pittsburgh's growing steel industry.

Butler soon had a steel business of its own thanks to the new railroad and the line became a conduit for iron ore. It became part of the Pennsylvania Railroad in 1903 and was abandoned in 1987. The trail opened in 1989.

The southern half of the Butler-Freeport Community Trail is nestled in a scenic wooded valley which follows Little Buffalo Creek to Buffalo Creek. Buffalo Creek then flows into the Allegheny River at Freeport. Remains of two stone quarries and some brick kilns can be seen in this southern section.

Heading north from Cabot, the results of late 19th century development are still visible. The former Saxon City Hotel, built in 1871, remains, as does an old, still active, lumberyard.

The middle segment, which was once rendered unusable due to trail access disputes, is now officially open after a long legal battle in local courts — thanks greatly to local trail advocates who labored tirelessly in and out of court to preserve this community asset.

From Pittsburgh, take Route 28 north to a left on Route 356 north. Go about four miles to Sarver Road. Bear right and go one mile to Buffalo Township. The fire station is on left. Park in the upper lot. This access area is three miles from the southern end and seven miles from the northern end of the trail.

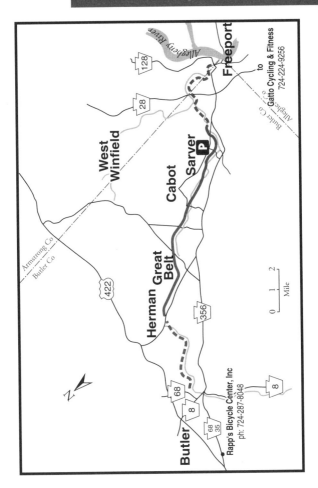

Location: Butler County
Miles: 12
Endpoints: Butler to Freeport
Surface: Crushed limestone
Contact: Ronald J. Bennett
Butler-Freeport Community
Trail Council, Inc.
PO Box 533
Saxonburg, PA 16056
724 -352-4783

Capital Area Greenbelt and Walnut Street Bridge

Harrisburg, Pennsylvania's Capital Area Greenbelt is a 20-mile ring of parks and trails encircling the City. Originally conceived by landscape architect Warren Manning (a disciple of Frederick Law Olmsted), the Greenbelt was partially constructed in accordance with Manning's plan through the early part of the 1900s. Unfortunately, the project was never fully realized and much of the Greenbelt fell into disuse and disrepair. In 1991, a group of dedicated volunteers took up the banner for park and trail development and formed the Capital Area Greenbelt Association.

An integral part of the Capital Area Greenbelt is the Walnut Street Bridge, which provides a critical pedestrian link to City Island. City Island is a popular multi-use recreational area in the heart of Harrisburg.

Built in 1889, the Walnut Street Bridge was used as a street car system that survived until 1950, when it was converted to automobile use. In 1972, Hurricane Agnes damaged the bridge beyond repair, and it was converted into a pedestrian bridge. In 1996, icy flood waters washed away the western span of the bridge. Today RTC leads the way in an effort to restore the structure.

A small section of the Greenbelt lies on an abandoned rail corridor, its trains once serving the industries that lined Harrisburg's Susquehanna Riverfront. To reach this portion of the circular trail, travel South Cameron Street to True Temper's Jackson Manufacturing plant. The rail-trail runs along South Cameron.

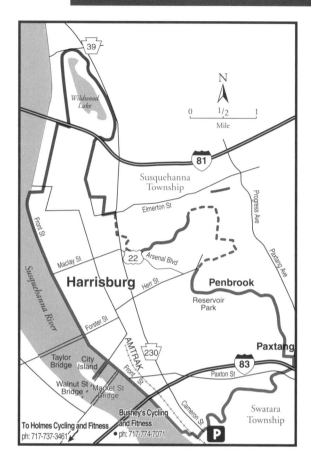

Location: Dauphin County
Miles: 20, about 2 miles on railroad corridor
Endpoints: Harrisburg — loop
Surface: Varied: wood chips, asphalt, stone and grass
Contact: Glenn Grimm
Capital Area Greenbelt Association
P.O. Box 15405
Harrisburg, PA 17105-5405
717-921-GREEN

Chester Valley Trail

Formed in 1850 by the Philadelphia and Reading Company, the Chester Valley Railroad stretched 22 miles between Bridgeport and Downingtown. The Chester Valley Trail follows the now-abandoned rail corridor and will soon reconnect Downingtown's Struble Trail with Montgomery County's Schuylkill River and new Perkiomen Creek trails. In the process, the trail will connect Downingtown's four parks, Chester County's major commercial center at Exton, and parks in East and West Whitehead Townships with Valley Forge National Park and further!

On National Trails Day 2000, Chester County Parks and Recreation officially opened a 1.4-mile demonstration section of the Chester Valley Trail. The demonstration section offers a relaxing route through one of Chester County's busiest areas. Plans to develop additional sections of trail continue with Phase One to extend from the Exton Park east to Merion Township and Phase Two to extend west to Downingtown.

In addition to providing recreation opportunities, the trail also provides transportation options; with prime access to a SEPTA line, the trail will offer commuters the choice to explore multimodal options.

Due to current construction and development, the trail is in various states of closure, so call before traveling.

To access the Chester Valley Trail take the PA Turnpike to Exit 23. Follow Rt. 100 south to Swedesford Road. Go left on Swedesford Road approximately 2.75 miles to Phoenixville Pike. Go left on Phoenixville Pike and travel about a quarter mile to trailhead parking at Battle of the Clouds Park on the right.

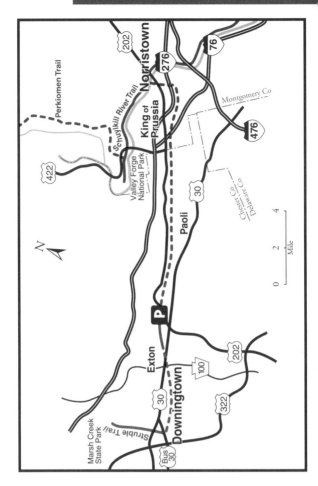

Location: Chester County
Miles: 1.4 miles
Endpoints: Downingtown to Norristown
Surface: Crushed limestone
Contact: Chester County Parks and Recreation
601 Westtown Road — Suite 160
P.O. Box 2747
West Chester, PA 19380-0990
610-344-6415
www.chesco.org/ccparks

Clarion Highlands Trail

The Clarion Highlands Trail is one of the highest rail-trails in the Commonwealth. It lies atop the Allegheny Plateau passing over the divide between the Clarion and Allegheny Rivers, and follows the Old Clarion Secondary Rail Corridor. It reaches a maximum elevation of 1472 feet at Phipps Cemetery near Elmo. Partly because of its elevation, average summer high temperatures are usually five degrees cooler than in Pittsburgh.

The AVTA holds a 25 ft. recreational trail easement on the westernmost mile of the rail bed, and owns the eastern five miles outright. All non-motorized uses are permitted on the eastern five miles of trail while horseback riding is prohibited on the western mile of trail. The trail corridor varies from 40 to 200 feet wide. In addition there are 20 acres of adjacent land where nature trails will be developed.

This trail/greenway also connects Gamelands No. 45 near Kossuth and No. 63 near Shippenville. The Game Commission has a purchase agreement to buy the rail bed within those areas. Thus, the old Clarion Secondary rail corridor has been preserved from Shippenville to the Allegheny River at Belmar.

A number of bridges over township roads have been removed. In these places, the rail bed has been graded back to a 2:1 slope, so care must be taken going up and down. At Phipps Cemetery the railroad has been filled. To the west an access ramp has been built courtesy of the Miles Construction Company.

The trail is located just north of US 322, paralleling that highway for six miles. It is easily accessed at the intersection of the Fern Road and US 322 near Elmo. More scenic sections may be reached via the following township roads: Knight Town Road: 2.6 miles west of the Shippenville traffic light, then one mile north. Pine City Road: 3.1 miles west of the Shippenville traffic light, then 1 mile north. Coal Hill Road at Kossuth: 6.7 miles west of the Shippenville traffic light, then 0.6 miles north.

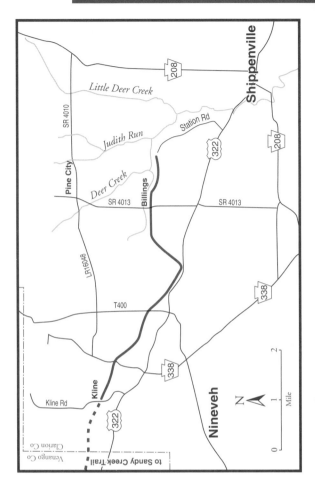

Location: Clarion
Miles: 6
Endpoints: Kline to Station Road
Surface: Gravel/dirt
Contact: David Howes
Allegheny Valley Trails Association
153 Sixth Ave.
Clarion, PA 16214
814-226-6455
Email: avta@clarion.edu
Web: http://avta-trails.org

Clarion-Little Toby Creek Trail

The Clairon-Little Toby Creek Rail-Trail is an 18-mile section of an abandoned rail line built by the Clearfield to Ridgway Rail Company. Built in 1886, the rail line was created to transport lumber and coal from mills to markets, but it also included a busy passenger service between Ridgway and Falls Creek. Abandoned in the 1960s, the corridor remained fairly intact under the ownership of Penn Central Corporation. Since 1992, the Tri-County Rails to Trails Association have been busy developing the abandoned line into one of the state's most beautiful rail-trails.

The trail meanders along the wild and scenic Clarion River and Little Toby Creek through Elk and Jefferson Counties, between the charming small towns of Ridgway and Brockway. Historical markers along the banks of the Little Toby Creek greet the trail user. These markers commemorate a former stone quarry in which a World War I munitions plant once stood, a Depression-era Civilian Conservation Corps camp which employed 250 men during the lean years of the 1930s, and a number of long-gone ghost towns from the lumbering era. Another fine feature of the trail is a swinging bridge across Little Toby Creek.

Ten miles of the trail are surfaced with crushed limestone, and the remainder is well graded with a cinder base. Funding is in place to complete improvements during 2002.

To reach the Brockway trailhead from I-80 Exit 97, take SR 219 North into Brockway. Turn left on Main Street. Turn right on 7th Avenue. The trailhead is at the end of the street, past the community pool. To reach the Ridgway trailhead from I-80, take SR 219 North to Ridgway. Turn left on Water Street, just before Love's Canoe and Market Basket. Continue one block to the trailhead, which is behind the Ridgway Record on Center Street.

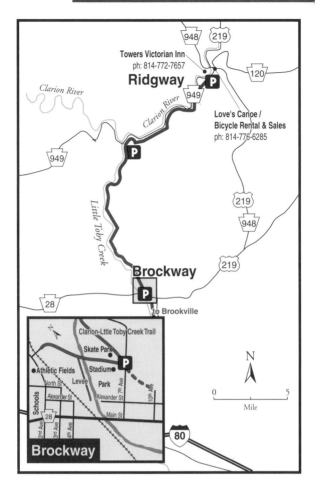

Location: Elk and Jefferson Counties

Miles: 18

Endpoints: Ridgway to Brockway

Surface: Crushed limestone & graded cinder

Contact: Ridgway Chamber of Commerce
231 Main St.
Ridgway, PA 15853
814-776-1424

Clearfield to Grampian Trail

By the mid-1860s the residents of isolated Clearfield County knew that the health of their economy was inexorably tied to the railroad. If the area's abundant coal was to reach distant metropolitan markets, their dependence upon wagons and shallow rivers had to shift. The Tyrone & Clearfield Railroad reached the county's border in 1863, but it wasn't until the Pennsylvania Railroad acquired the TCR in 1866 that a connection seemed possible. An association of 75 volunteers was formed to try to extend the railroad to the county seat. In three years the association raised $77,000 and in January 1869 the first train arrived in Clearfield. By Christmas Day 1874, similar efforts in Curwensville brought train service west. It took 18 more years for the railroad to reach Grampian.

Today this hard won corridor is the Clearfield to Grampian Trail. From Clearfield to Curwensville the trail follows the West Branch of the Susquehanna River near the Curwensville Lake Recreation Area, with modern camping facilities and a beach for watersports. After leaving Curwensville and traveling southwest to Grampian, the terrain becomes more densely forested, bridging Anderson Creek next to an old time swimming hole and traveling along Kratzer Run to the small town of Grampian. The final section of the trail was completed in 1998, and the trail now consists of 10.5 miles of crushed limestone surface suitable for road bikes and wheelchairs.

To reach the Clearfield trailhead, take I-80 to Exit 120 (Clearfield). Take PA 879 South about 2.5 miles and turn right on the Spruce Street exit. Take the first left (Chester Street) and in another 200 yards turn left just before the True Value Hardware store. The trailhead is just ahead on the left. Parking is available at the Riverside supermarket nearby during the week; park at the trailhead on weekends.

The Grampian trailhead is just one block from the town's only stoplight at the intersection of US219, PA879 and PA729. A large sign on PA729 identifies the trailhead / public parking area.

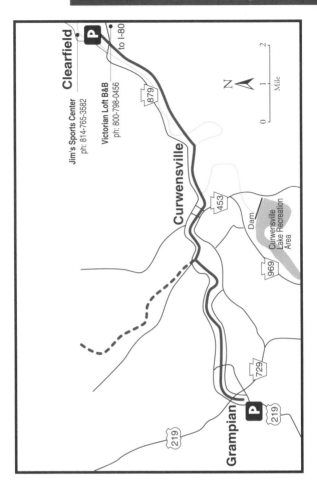

Location: Clearfield County

Miles: 10.5

Endpoints: Clearfield to Grampian

Surface: Crushed limestone

Contact: Fredric J. Ammerman
Clearfield County Rails-to-Trails
310 East Cherry Street
Clearfield, PA 16830
814-765-1701

Conewago Trail

Built in 1883 by Robert H. Coleman, who was one of the richest men in America at the time, the Cornwall & Lebanon Railroad operated for almost 100 years. This privately owned railroad served the Coleman family well by transporting iron from the family's iron furnaces to the Pennsylvania Railroad, which would then haul the iron ore to the mill at Steelton.

By 1910, there were eight daily passenger trains to the resort town of Mt. Gretna, home of the Pennsylvania Chautauqua and the National Guard encampment. The tracks were abandoned after the Hurricane Agnes flood of 1972, and converted into a trail in 1981.

Shaded by a canopy of trees, the Conewago Trail is a wonderful way to spend your day, whether you like to horseback ride, walk, jog, or bicycle.

Starting out, you will pass the quiet and meandering Conewago Creek, fields of corn, and open meadows. Not long into your journey, you will hear rushing water as you approach a wide creek and large boulders. This is an ideal spot to take a break and listen to the water and watch the swirling rapids.

Continuing, you will pass through some pockets of wooded land where you may see deer or grouse. You will also pass a few horse, dairy, and chicken farms. Diverse and peaceful, this trail is the perfect escape.

The most conveniently located trailhead is along Route 230, two miles west of Elizabethtown.

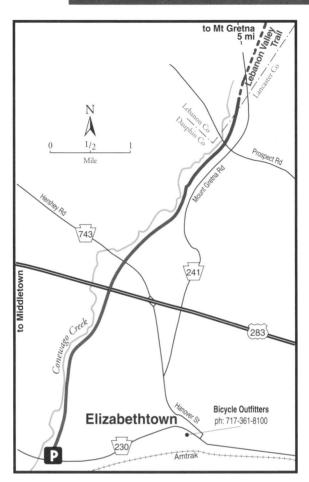

Location: Lancaster County
Miles: 5
Endpoints: Conewago to Cornwall
Surface: Cinder
Contact: Lancaster County Parks & Recreation
1050 Rockford Road
Lancaster, PA 17602
717-295-3605

Conservancy Narrow Gauge Rail Trail

Eagles Mere, located at 2100 feet in the Endless Mountains of Northeast Pennsylvania, is a town rich with history dating back over 200 years. In 1794 George Lewis bought the lake and surrounding land, and erected a glass factory which operated until the end of the War of 1812. In the late 1800s, the town served as the true logging capital of the world.

In 1892 the Eagles Mere Railroad was built between Sonestown and Eagles Mere. At Sonestown it connected with the Williamsport and North Branch. The railroad stretched eight miles, and in 1904 was extended around the lake at Eagles Mere Park. Through the roaring 1920s, excursion service to Eagles Mere offered the wealthy a peaceful escape from the hustle and bustle of large cities like Philadelphia. The Eagles Mere Railroad garnered praise as one of most scenic lines in the state. While in transit along the Eagles Mere Railroad, passengers marveled at the wildflowers and waterfalls along the route.

Today, Eagles Mere continues to offer a place of escape. And the abandoned Eagles Mere Railroad offers a peaceful path of 1.6 miles connecting to more than 100 additional miles of trail throughout Wyoming State Forest. Linking with trails ranging from easy to singletrack, the Conservancy Narrow Gauge Rail-Trail provides trail users with a great place to begin an adventure.

Regardless of the route chosen, natural splendor will follow — an easy walk along the rail-trail from the trailhead provides gorgeous views of the spring-fed Eagles Mere Lake, while a more challenging jaunt off the rail-trail along singletrack leads to the waterfall pictured above.

To access the Conservancy Narrow Gauge Rail-Trail from Williamsport, travel US 220 northeast through the towns of Picture Rocks and Strawbridge. In Muncy Valley go left and head north on PA 42. Follow PA approximately 6 miles to Eagles Mere. Continue through town to the lily pond and trailhead parking.

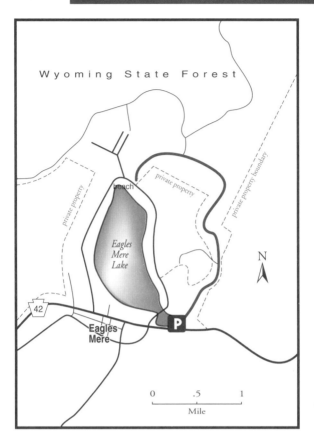

Wyoming State Forest

private property

private property

private property boundary

beach

Eagles Mere Lake

N

42

Eagles Mere

P

0 .5 1
Mile

Location:	Sullivan County
Miles:	1.6
Endpoints:	Lilly Pond to Eagles Mere Park
Surface:	Unimproved/Unmaintainted
Contact:	Eagles Mere Conservancy
	P.O. Box 64
	Eagles Mere, PA 17731
	570-525-3725

Cumberland County Hiker/Biker Trail

South Mountain in Pennsylvania actually marks the northern end of the mighty Blue Ridge chain, which stretches south to Georgia. Pine Grove Furnace first began operating in 1764 to take advantage of the relatively small but rich South Mountain iron ore deposits.

Exactly 100 years after the furnace began, the South Mountain Railroad was built to serve it. After iron-making ceased, the railroad eked out a living hauling slate, sand and tourists. Starting in 1940, the line was abandoned in segments.

The state forestry department purchased the furnace property in 1911, and it ultimately became Michaux State Forest and Pine Grove Furnace State Park.

About 30,000 people use the Cumberland County Hiker/ Biker Trail each year. The trail begins near Fuller Lake, which was originally an iron ore pit, and passes relics of the iron-making era: the ironmaster's house, the furnace remains, the original company store, stable, grist mill, and inn - now the park office.

Pine Grove marks the halfway point of the Appalachian Trail, which crosses the valley at each end of the Cumberland County Hiker / Biker Trail and accommodates foot traffic only. The quarter-mile-long Swamp nature trail and the steep Pole Steeple Trail with its spectacular view of the entire 696-acre park create a trail network with a variety of hiking possibilities.

From I-81, take Exit 37 and proceed south on Route 233 to the state park. Park at the Iron Furnace's stack pavilion and proceed east to the trailhead.

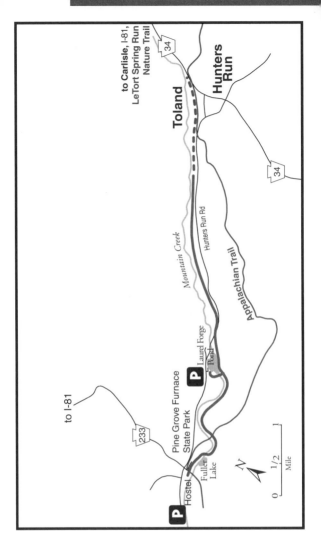

Location:	Cumberland County
Miles:	5.5
Endpoints:	Pine Grove Furnace State Park to Mountain Creek Campground
Surface:	Crushed limestone / asphalt
Contact:	Pine Grove Furnace State Park
	1100 Pine Grove Road
	Gardners, PA 17324
	717-486-7174
	www.dcnr.state.pa.us

Cumberland Valley Rail-Trail

Headquartered in Lemoyne, the Cumberland Valley Railroad was first incorporated in 1831. The railroad was ahead of its time, running the first sleeping car in the nation and instituting one of the first prohibitions against drug and alcohol use by its employees.

The same sense of pride and close-knit community spirit that led CVRR foremen to offer cash prizes to any child who found so much as a stone out of place along the rail line now guides the Cumberland Valley Rails-to-Trails Council as it works to establish its trail along 11 miles of the CVRR corridor. Not even demolition of four historic concrete arch bridges can temper the group's determination to reconnect the towns of Shippensburg and Newville. The trail is presently undeveloped and suitable for walking, mountain biking and equestrian use only. Because of the steep embankments caused by the loss of the bridges, some road crossings require extra caution on the part of trail users. Engineering for improvements continues and construction will follow.

The best access to the trail is at Oakville. From US 11 or PA533, turn west on Oakville Road into the village. Turn left at Beidler Drive and park adjacent to grassy picnic area. The trail crosses Oakville Road along the west side of the picnic area.

For access in Newville, Take I81 to Exit 37 — PA 233. Take PA 233 south to PA533 — 2.5 past the intersection with US 11. Head west on PA 533, through the stop sign, and take a left on Cherry Street. Continue to McFarland Street and park along the south/east side of McFarland.

Hikers may park at the Shippensburg municipal lot on West Burd Street; however, there is no equestrian or bicycle access in Shippensburg at this time.

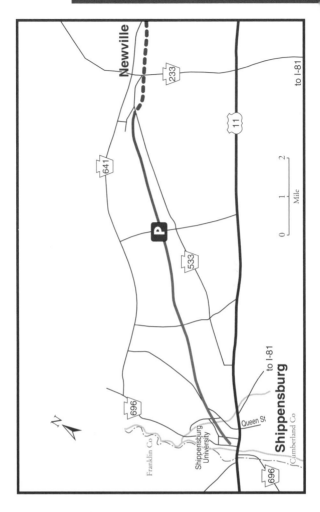

Location: Cumberland County
Miles: 11
Endpoints: Shippensburg to Newville
Surface: Dirt, grass, original ballast (to be improved)
Contact: Jerry Angulo
Cumberland Valley Rails-to-Trails Council
PO Box 531
Shippensburg, PA 17257
717-263-1713

**Equestrian
Contact:** Diane Morrow
717-352-7687

D & H Rail-Trail

In August 1829, the Delaware & Hudson Gravity Railroad conducted a trial test of the first steam locomotive to operate in the United States. Built in England, the "Stourbridge Lion" traveled an astonishing three miles from Honesdale to Seeleyville when its operators discovered it was too heavy for the track. By 1830, the 17 miles of the D&H Railroad constituted the vast majority of railroad mileage in the United States—23 whole miles!

From these small beginnings, shipping anthracite coal and lumber from Carbondale to Honesdale, the Delaware & Hudson became a successful mining and railroad company. By 1870, hard coal from the rich mines of the Lackawanna Valley was rolling north out of Carbondale to points all over the northeastern United States and Canada on the D&H line that became the trail.

Paralleling the Lackawanna River and the O&W Rail-Trail (see page 114) for several miles, the D&H Rail-Trail offers scenic vistas of the river corridor: waterfalls, clear pools and rhododendron-lined banks. Usable by hikers, mountain bikers, snowmobilers, and cross-country skiers, the D&H Rail-Trail is already a vital resource for the communities of northeastern Pennsylvania. Currently the trail tread is quite rugged along the entire length of the trail. So expect rough going.

To reach Simpson, take I-81 to Exit 185, then Route 6 to Carbondale. After the town of Carbondale, turn left onto Route 171. Continue about one mile, park on right side of viaduct in Simpson. Follow the O&W Trail for one mile, where it accesses the D&H to the west.

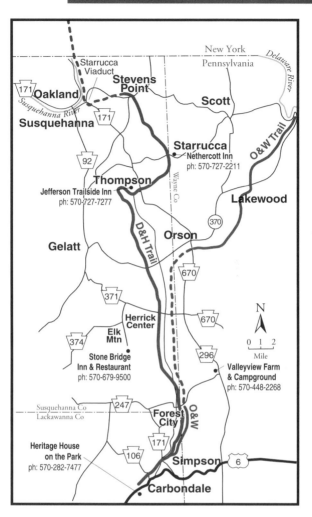

Location: Lackawanna, Wayne and Susquehanna
Counties
Miles: 32
Endpoints: Simpson to Stevens Point
Surface: Cinder, original ballast (to be resurfaced)
Contact: Lynn Conrad
Rail-Trail Council of N.E. Pennsylvania
PO Box 123
Forest City, PA 18421-0123
570-785-7245

43

Delaware Canal Towpath

The Delaware Canal is the only remaining continuously intact canal of the great canal-building era of the early and mid 1800s. Through the connection with the Lehigh Navigation Canal at Easton, the Delaware Canal helped to develop the anthracite coal industry in the Upper Lehigh Valley. The U.S. Congress officially recognized the canal's importance to the economic evolution of America by establishing the Delaware & Lehigh National Heritage Corridor in 1988.

Even before the canal closed to commercial activity, many people used the waterway for recreational purposes. Since becoming a state park in 1940, people have visited the canal to fish and canoe. Today the 60-mile Delaware Canal Towpath, once trod by teams of mules pulling cargo-laden boats, also serves walkers, joggers, bikers, cross country skiers, bird watchers and equestrians.

For 30 miles the Delaware Canal Towpath parallels the D&R Canal Towpath. With six bridges crossing the mighty Delaware River and linking the two trails, users can choose from many possible routes to enjoy the trails and the adjacent towns.

Resurfacing during the spring of 2002 will upgrade the surface to crushed stone.

To access the trail in Washington Crossing, take I-95 exit number 51 towards New Hope. Stay left off the exit and merge onto Taylorsville Road. Travel approximately 3 miles to Taylorsville and take a right onto PA 532. Pass General Knox and General Sutton roads, and take a left on River Road / PA 32. Park in lot on left.

From U.S. 22 take 25th Street South (1.6 miles) to Lehigh Drive, turn right and go .5 mile to stop sign. Turn right at entrance bridge to Hugh Moore Park. Cross the bridge, then go right and park near the picnic area.

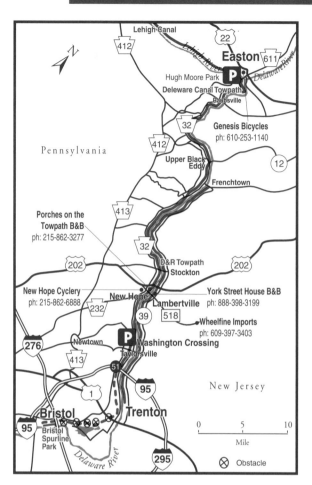

Lehigh Canal
412
22
Easton
611
Hugh Moore Park
Deleware Canal Towpath
Raubsville
32
Genesis Bicycles
ph: 610-253-1140
412
12
Upper Black
Eddy
P e n n s y l v a n i a
Frenchtown
413
**Porches on the
Towpath B&B**
ph: 215-862-3277
32
202
D&R Towpath
Stockton
202
New Hope Cyclery
ph: 215-862-6888
232
New Hope
York Street House B&B
ph: 888-398-3199
Lambertville
39
518
Wheelfine Imports
ph: 609-397-3403
276
Newtown
Washington Crossing
413
Taylorsville
51
New Jersey
1
95
0   5   10
Mile
Bristol
95
Trenton
Bristol
Spurline
Park
Delaware River
295
⊗ Obstacle

Location:	Northampton and Bucks counties
Miles:	60
Endpoints:	Easton to Bristol
Surface:	Dirt / crushed stone
Contact:	Delaware Canal State Park
	11 Lodi Hill Road
	Upper Black Eddy, PA 18972
	610-982-5560
	delawaresp@a1.dcnr.state.pa.us

Eliza Furnace Trail

Laughlin and Company built two of the famous Eliza Furnaces in 1861. The famous Jones and Laughlin Steel Company was formed in 1902 when Benjamin Franklin Jones, owner of an interest in the American Iron Works and Laughlin Steel Company, merged with Laughlin Steel. In keeping with Victorian tradition, furnaces were named after women because they were considered fickle and temperamental. One of Jones' granddaughters was named Eliza. The Jones and Laughlin Steel Company at its peak occupied over 750 acres and seven miles of riverfront along the Ohio and Monogahela Rivers and employed 30,000 at its facilities. The Hot Metal Bridge carried iron by rail from the Eliza furnaces to the Southside where finished steel was produced and shipped. As the Big Steel Industry changed, the Eliza furnaces were shut down on June 22, 1979. They were replaced by two electric furnaces on the Southside. In 1983, "Anna," the last of the Eliza furnaces was demolished. Today the Pittsburgh Technology Center sits were the furnaces were once located.

The first phase of the trail extends from Grant Street at 1st Avenue to Swinburne Street and is 2.5 miles long. Phase Two extends the trail through Panther Hollow and up to Schenley Park and Oakland. The trail was constructed by the City of Pittsburgh's Department of Public Works. Highlights along the trail include spectacular views of the Monongahela River, the Pittsburgh Technology Center, and the Southside and the Southside Slopes neighborhoods.

To access the trail from downtown Pittsburgh, turn off Grant Street behind the PNC Firstside Building directly onto the trail at 1st Avenue.

To access the trail from the end of the first phase, take 2nd Avenue and turn onto Swinburne Street, which is very close to the Hot Metal Bridge. Free parking is available at Swinburne Street.

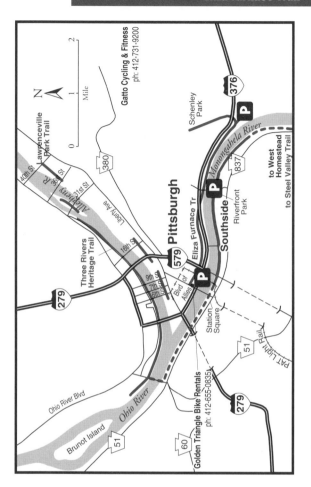

Location: Allegheny County
Miles: 4
Endpoints: Grant Street to Swinburne St.
Surface: 10 foot wide asphalt path with crushed lime-
stone on either side
Contact: Office of the Mayor
414 Grant Street
Room 512, City County Building
Pittsburgh, PA 15219
412-255-2626

Endless Mountain Riding Trail

It pays to have friends in high places, or so the story goes for the Endless Mountain Trail. A retired judge living in Montrose in 1943 had such a friend. The judge, a former World War I cavalryman, was involved in a local riding club and happened to have a very good friend who worked for the Delaware, Lackawanna & Western Railroad. When the Montrose Branch was abandoned in 1944, the judge's friend sold it to him for one dollar, creating a trail for the riding club and one of the nation's first rail-trails. After enjoying the trail for many years, the original members of the club gave the right-of-way to the Bridgewater Riding Club, which has continued the trail's tradition.

Heavily forested for much of its length, this very rugged trail begins near a golf course and passes by many farms and rural homes. Along the way, you will enjoy a 60-foot waterfall, intact railroad ties alongside the trail, and an old railroad depot. You may also hear or see a woodpecker if you're lucky! Although perfect for horseback riding, the trail is also used for mountain biking and hiking, and is home to a 10k race every July 4th.

The trail starts behind the Humane Society facility in Montrose. Take Route 706 (Grow Avenue) in Montrose to the Society and park there. Accessing the trail near Alford is presently confusing and should be avoided.

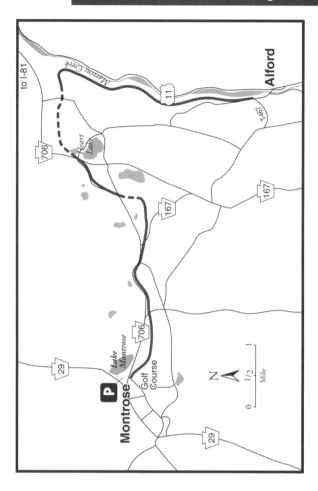

Location: Susquehanna County
Miles: 14
Endpoints: Alford to Montrose
Surface: Original ballast
Contact: Tom Wooden
Center for Anti-Slavery Studies
2 Maple Street
Montrose, PA 18801
570-278-0277

Ernst Bike Trail

The Meadville-Linesville Railroad was built from 1880-1892 by a group of Meadville entrepreneurs to gain access to the Pennsylvania Railroad at Linesville. Despite the involvement of some of Meadville's best-known citizens, the railroad did not flourish.

In 1891, the Bessemer & Lake Erie Railroad Company leased the right-of-way and for a time the most profitable use was as a passenger line, transporting visitors to Exposition Park (renamed Conneaut Lake Park in 1920). With the rise of the automobile, passenger service declined and in 1934 rail service to the park was discontinued. The Bessemer abandoned the line in 1976. In 1996, Calvin Ernst, the right-of-way's owner, donated the property to French Creek Recreational Trails and the Ernst Bike Trail was born.

Traversing terrain with imprints of Ice Age glaciations, the trail passes through the lush bottom lands of French Creek Valley. With 66 species of fish and 27 species of mollusks, French Creek is Pennsylvania's most biologically diverse body of water. From the creek to the end of the trail's completed portion, the landscape is pastoral with varied environments of meadow and marsh, hardwood stands and hemlock thickets. The proposed segment from Route 19 to Conneaut Lake parallels Conneaut Marsh, an ancient river valley infield with glacial debris, and home to nesting bald eagles and migrating waterfowl.

The trail is currently accessed at its middle, located at the track crossing on Old Mercer Pike. The distance in either direction is approximately 2.5 miles.

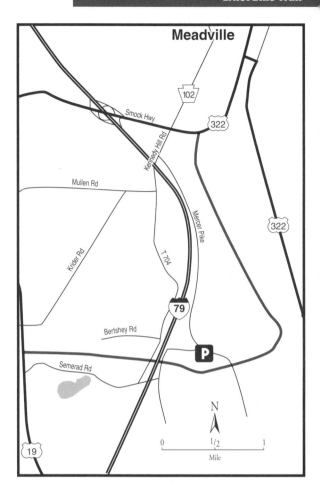

Meadville

102

322

Smock Hwy

Kennedy Hill Rd

322

Mullen Rd

Mercer Pike

Krider Rd

T-704

79

Bertshey Rd

P

Semerad Rd

19

N

| 0 | 1/2 | 1 |

Mile

Location: Crawford County
Miles: 5
Endpoints: Meadville to Route 19
Surface: Crushed stone
Contact: John Wallach
French Creek Recreational Trails, Inc.
c/o Community Health Services
747 Terrace Street
Meadville, PA 16335
814-333-2063

Five Star Trail

The Five Star Trail is a "Rail-with-Trail" located along the Southwest Pennsylvania Railroad corridor between Greensburg and Youngwood, in central Westmoreland County. This 6.6-mile trail begins at the Lynch Field Recreation complex, located off Route 119 North in Greensburg and travels south to the Westmoreland County Community College in Youngwood. It is a non-motorized recreational trail for walking, jogging, bicycling and cross country skiing, as well as an alternative transportation resource for residents of central Westmoreland County. Trail visitors may wish to stop in at the Youngwood Trail Station, a small museum that focuses on local railroad history. The rail corridor was purchased from Conrail in 1995 by the Westmoreland County Industrial Development Corporation. The rail is operated by the Southwest Pennsylvania Railroad and provides freight service through central Westmoreland County. The trail is being managed by the Five Star Trail Chapter of the Regional Trail Corporation. The name "Five Star" comes from the five municipalities that joined forces to construct and manage the trail: City of Greensburg, Hempfield Township, and the Boroughs of Youngwood, South Greensburg, and Southwest Greensburg.

For trail access in Greensburg, take US 30 to Route 119. Follow Route 119 north, winding through town 1.9 miles to the Lynch Field Recreation Complex — which is about .5 miles past the Stereo Shop.

To access the trail from the south, take US 30 to Route 119. Follow Route 119 south, passing Hoss's, 2.2 miles to Trolley Line Road and trailhead parking.

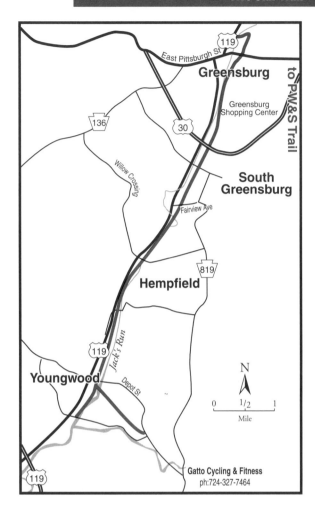

Greensburg Shopping Center

East Pittsburgh St

Greensburg

to PW&S Trail

South Greensburg

Willow Crossing

Fairview Ave

Hempfield

Jack's Run

Youngwood

Depot St

N

0   1/2   1
Mile

Gatto Cycling & Fitness
ph:724-327-7464

Location:	Westmoreland County
Miles:	6.6
Endpoints:	Greensburg to Youngwood
Surface:	Crushed limestone and asphalt
Contact:	Malcom N. Sias
	Five Star Trail Chapter
	R.R. #12, Box 203
	Greensburg, PA 15601
	724-830-3962

Forks Township Recreation Trail

Traveling as it does through cornfields and woodlands, the Forks Township Recreation Trail feels like a quiet country lane. The trail meanders past old stone fencing and rocky outcrops and passes high above the Delaware River. It's a welcome respite for local workers who often take their lunch breaks along its quiet pathway.

Built by the Lehigh & New England Railroad, the corridor connected at Martins Creek with the Delaware, Lackawanna & Western Railroad. The DL&W was one of northeastern Pennsylvania's largest railroads and its network of railroad corridors forms the backbone of rail-trail construction in this area of the state.

Take Exit 6 (13th Street) from Route 22 in Easton and turn left at stoplight onto 13th Street. At the next traffic light (Bushkill Drive) turn left. After three miles, turn right onto Newlins Road West and then left at Sullivan Trail. Make a quick right turn back onto Newlins Road West. At the intersection with Broadway, turn right and follow Broadway .2 miles to the trailhead.

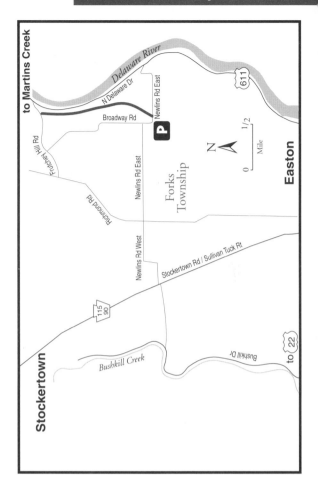

Location: Northampton County
Miles: 1.5
Endpoints: Uhlers Station to Frutchey Hill Road
Surface: Asphalt
Contact: Forks Township
1606 Sullivan Trail
Easton, PA 18040
610-252-0785

Ghost Town Trail

Five different railroads operated in the Blacklick Valley, most notably the Cambria & Indiana (originally the Blacklick and Yellow Creek, a logging railroad) and the Pennsylvania Railroad's Blacklick Secondary, the two lines that have become the Ghost Town Trail.

The lines once served eight coal mining towns, a lumbering town and mill, and three iron furnaces in the valley. Now all that marks this once-bustling industrial area are a few buildings and a lot of foundations.

Along the way, you'll pass woodlands and parallel Blacklick Creek. You'll find railroad bridges and creeks stocked with trout, abandoned mining towns, and the Eliza Iron Furnace, which is one of Pennsylvania's best preserved iron furnaces and a national historic site. You'll traverse state game land—home to a variety of wildlife, including bear, turkey, deer, and songbirds.

From points west: travel US22 through Blairsville to PA403 – two miles beyond the intersection with PA56. Follow 403 north one mile to the village of Dilltown. Park at the Dilltown Station located 360 feet beyond the bridge over Blacklick Creek.

From points east: travel US22 trough Holidaysburg to PA271 – four miles west of the intersection with US219. Follow 271 north one mile to the village of Nanty Glo. Take a left at the fire station and continue to trailhead parking.

For the Rexis Branch: travel US 22 through Blairsville to Wehrum Road -+– four miles beyond the intersection with PA56. Turn left on Wehrum Road and continue four miles to the trailhead – which offers immediate access to the Rexis Branch as well as the Ghost Town Trail.

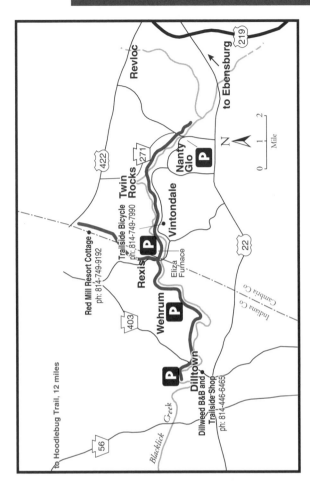

Location:	Cambria and Indiana Counties
Miles:	16
Endpoints:	Nanty Glo to Dilltown
Surface:	Crushed limestone
Contact:	Indiana County Parks
	Blue Spruce Park Rd
	Indiana, PA 15701
	724-463-8636
Contact:	Cambria County Conservation &
	Recreation Authority
	401 Candlelight Dr., Suite 234
	Ebensburg, PA 15931
	814-472-2110

Great Shamokin Path

Built as the Rural Valley Railroad, the Great Shamokin Path is named after the path that once linked the Allegheny and Susquehanna Rivers and ran from Kittanning to Sunbury. The Rural Valley Railroad eventually wound up in the hands of the Baltimore and Ohio, which abandoned the Yatesboro to NuMine section in 1964.

The line was purchased in 1984 by the Cowanshannock Creek Watershed Association, a non-profit volunteer organization dedicated to improving the water quality of the creek. Acquisition funds for the trail came from the granting of a water main easement under the trail. This type of joint use is increasingly popular as a means of rail-trail development.

This mostly grass-covered trail climbs steadily through the Cowanshannock Creek Valley past the Devil's Washbasin, a 1.5 acre lake named for its dam across the creek to obtain water for steam engines - always smoky, steamy and eerie looking. The lake is stocked with fish and offers ice fishing and picnicking.

Near the trail's upper end, White Lake and its adjacent wetlands were created in 1988 to improve water quality in the creek which had deteriorated because of acid mine drainage.

Go east on PA85, just north of Kittanning off PA28/66 to Yatesboro. The Valley Village Store is at the west end of Yatesboro. Just east of the store before the turnoff to Yatesboro, an unmarked lot on the right provides parking for the west trailhead. To reach the trailhead in NuMine, continue on PA85 about 3 miles east from Yatesboro. Turn right at the intersection where a left turn leads to NuMine. Immediately cross Cowanshannock Creek, turn right between the ballfield and the creek. A gated trailhead is just ahead, or you may drive a little farther to the White Lake picnic area.

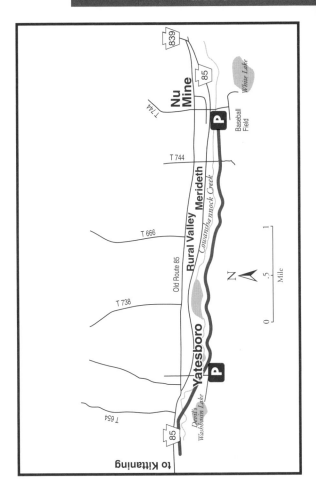

Location: Armstrong County
Miles: 4.5
Endpoints: Yatesboro to NuMine
Surface: Gravel, original ballast
Contact: Pam Meade
Cowanshannock Creek Watershed Association
PO Box 307
Rural Valley, PA 16249
724-783-6692

Heritage Rail Trail County Park

The Heritage Rail Trail County Park's 21 miles link with Maryland's Northern Central Rail Trail to provide a 40+ mile journey through southcenral Pennsylvania's and northcentral Maryland's farmlands and forests. With construction complete on the Segment from Hanover Junction to York, the HRTCP is now the longest non-motorized rail-with-trail in the United States.

The 19th century saw the growth of the Northern Central Railroad, a vital link between Washington, DC, Harrisburg, upstate New York and Lake Ontario. Its passage through York County brought prosperity to the area's farmers, merchants and manufacturers and spurred the growth of communities like Glen Rock, Hanover Junction and the aptly-named town of Railroad along winding Codorus Creek.

The railroad was also a prime target for the Confederate Army prior to the Battle of Gettysburg, as Rebel troops cut telegraph wires and destroyed bridges in their efforts to isolate Washington from the rest of the Union. After the tragic Battle, President Lincoln traveled via the Northern Central to the battlefield, his train stopping in Hanover Junction where Matthew Brady took a photograph showing, according to many, the President standing outside the station.

After the war, the railroad remained a vital link between the nation's prosperous cities. Passengers could leave York and make their way to Baltimore and Washington, DC to the south, Chicago and St. Louis to the west, and Buffalo and New York to the north.

Hanover Junction is located on SR616 north of Glen Rock. From Interstate 83, take Exit 10 (Loganville). Follow signs to 214. Continue west on 214 for approximately 5 miles to 616 South. Follow 616 South. The parking lot is approximately one mile on the left.

For parking in York, use Lafayette Plaza, 205 W. Market Street, which is behind the courthouse. Parking is free after 6 PM on weekdays and all weekend.

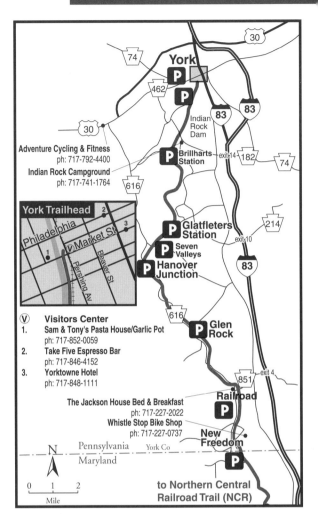

30

74

York

P

P

462

83

83

Indian Rock Dam

30

Adventure Cycling & Fitness
ph: 717-792-4400

Indian Rock Campground
ph: 717-741-1764

P **Brillharts Station**

exit 14

182

74

616

York Trailhead 2

Philadelphia

Market St

Beaver St

Pershing Av

1

3

P **Glatfleters Station**

exit 10

214

83

P **Seven Valleys**

P **Hanover Junction**

616

Ⓥ **Visitors Center**
1. **Sam & Tony's Pasta House/Garlic Pot**
   ph: 717-852-0059
2. **Take Five Espresso Bar**
   ph: 717-846-4152
3. **Yorktowne Hotel**
   ph: 717-848-1111

P **Glen Rock**

exit 4

851

The Jackson House Bed & Breakfast
ph: 717-227-2022

Whistle Stop Bike Shop
ph: 717-227-0737

Railroad

P

New Freedom

P

N

Pennsylvania   York Co

Maryland

0   1   2
Mile

to Northern Central Railroad Trail (NCR)

Location: York County
Miles: 21
Endpoints: York to Maryland border
Surface: Crushed limestone
Contact: York County Department of Parks
and Recreation
400 Mundis Race Rd.
York, PA 17402
717-840-7440

Hoodlebug Trail

The Hoodlebug Trail follows the abandoned Indiana Branch of the Pennsylvania Railroad. The line, completed in 1856, extended north from Blairsville to Indiana. 'Hoodlebug' was the local nickname given to the self-propelled passenger coach that ran on the line until 1940.

The trail corridor has played an important role in the region for many years: as part of an extensive network of Native American trails, as a PRR branch line, and now as a pedestrian and bicycle trail. The Hoodlebug Trail preserves this historically significant transportation corridor.

Today the trail — surfaced in part with highway millings provided by a partnership between Indiana County Parks and PennDOT District 10 — provides transportation options and recreational opportunities along the historic corridor. Recent improvements include a new 60-foot trail underpass. Future plans include connecting the Hoodlebug Trail to the proposed Route 119 Bikeway and the popular Ghost Town Trail.

Please be advised that two sections of the trail in Homer City are not complete, creating a .5 mile gap in the trail. These gaps can be connected using Borough streets. Construction will close the gaps in 2002. For users not familiar with Homer City, the IUP South Campus parking lot is recommended as it provides access to five continuous miles of trail.

To access the Hoodlebug Trail in Homer City: Homer City is located five miles south of Indiana. From PA Route 119, turn onto PA Route 56 West. Turn right onto Main Street in Homer City. Follow Main Street to Floodway Park. Parking area is on the right. Amenities include restrooms (closed during winter months), a pavilion, picnic tables, and a playground.

To access the trail at the Indiana University of Pennsylvania South Campus, Follow Rt 119 to the Wayne Avenue exit. At the third light, take a left on Rose Street — and notice the trailhead on the left just past Hoss's Restaurant. Turn left on Kolter, and then turn left on University Drive. Go past the first large parking lot and turn into the second — at the Continuing Ed Computer Lab. Park and return to Rose Street for access. Restrooms are available.

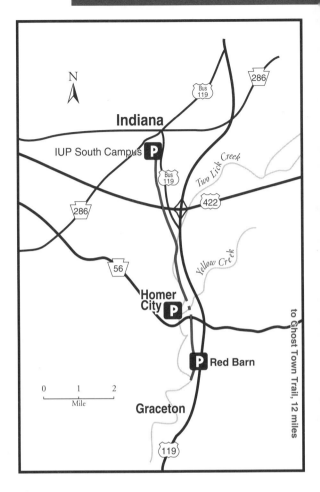

Location:	Indiana County
Miles:	6
Endpoints:	Indiana to Homer City
Surface:	Crushed stone
Contact:	Indiana County Parks
	1128 Blue Spruce Rd
	Indiana, PA 15701
	724-463-8636
	email: indparks@stargate.net
	website: www.indianacountyparks.org

Houtzdale Line Trail

The old railroad line known as the "Moshannon" or the "Mills" branch crossed the Moshannon Valley during the middle to late 1800s, transporting the valley's coal deposits. The line was the foundation of the region's late 19th and early 20th century economy. The history of coal mining in the area is noticeable from the trail as it passes remnants of the industry. Interpretive signage will soon commemorate particularly important historical structures and event sites along the trail.

Purchased from Conrail in 1994 following abandonment, the corridor was converted to a multi-use path in order to preserve the land as a public asset. The entire length of the Houtzdale Line Trail is open for use. The trail has been graded and compacted. The cinder and mowed sod surface is suitable for hiking, mountain biking, skiing, and equestrian use. The eight mile section between SR2005 at Smoke Run and SR2007 just east of Houtzdale is in the best condition. The extreme east end of the trail is in a rough condition due to utility construction and erosion.

The trail is surrounded by private property, so please do respect the rights of the property owners.

To reach Houtzdale from I-99, take 453N to Viola. Take 153N to Houtzdale. On street parking is available throughout Houtzdale, and off-street parking is available behind the Bilo supermarket on Rt 53 east of Houtzdale.

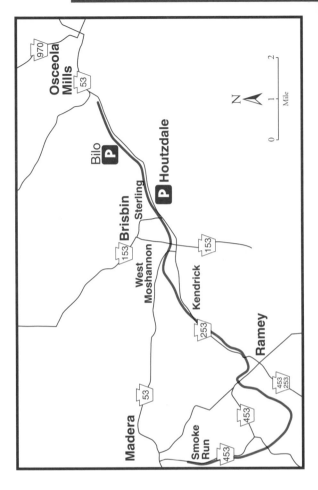

Location: Clearfield County
Miles: 10.5
Endpoints: Smoke Run (SR 2005) to Houtzdale
Surface: Crushed stone, (Houtzdale to Smoke Run) cinder and grass
Contact: Dennis Kasubik
501 David St.
Houtzdale, PA 16651
814-378-7817

Indian Creek Valley Trail

The Indian Creek Valley Railroad (ICVRR) was built in Indian Head in 1906, and extended to Jones Mill, near Donegal, by the time it was finished in 1910. The ICVRR continued to operate until 1926, carrying passengers and freight to meet the Baltimore and Ohio Railroad (B&O) at the juncture of Indian Creek and the Youghiogheny River. The B&O bought the ICVRR and continued operating the main line until 1972, when it was completely abandoned. The Western Pennsylvania Conservancy then acquired the corridor and offered it to Saltlick Township, which opened the trail in 1989.

Perfect for hiking and mountain biking, the Indian Creek Valley Trail is a great escape from the crowds in the nearby Ohiopyle area. The right-of-way continues south to the Youghiogheny River and could one day be linked with the Youghiogheny River Trail.

To access the trail in Champion, take the PA Turnpike to Exit 91 at Donegal, From the toll plaza, take a left on Route 31 East, passing Hardees, and travel 2 miles and go right at Sarnelli's Market on Route 381/711. Travel one mile and take a left just past the county line and just before the Starz Market. Park less than a quarter mile down the road on the left behind the Champion Station Coffee Shop and hit the trail across the street.

Nearby in Forbes State Forest and Linn Run State Park, the PW&S Railroad Hiking-Biking Trail offers 9.5 miles of dirt trail.

To access the PW&S Trail at Linn Run Road, go east from Greensburg on US30. Go 2 miles past Ligonier and at PA381 turn right. Go 3 miles to Linn Run Road in Rector. Turn left onto Linn Run Rd, travel 4 miles to the start of Quarry Trail, and park in parking lot. You can follow Linn Run Rd to the top of the mountain, and try the Beam Run Trail.

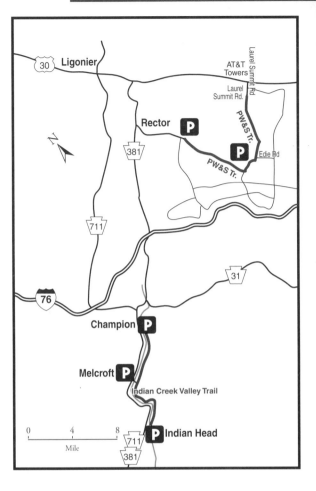

Location: Fayette County
Miles: 5
Endpoints: Champion to Indian Head
Surface: Crushed aggregate
Contact: Saltlick Township
PO Box 403
Melcroft, PA 15462
724-455-2866

Iron Horse Trail

This trail follows two abandoned railbeds, the Path Valley Railroad and the Perry Lumber Company Railroad. The Path Valley Railroad was never completed due to financial and construction problems. Originally, it was going to be an extension for the Newport and Shermans Valley Railroad and would end in Hancock, Maryland. After the grade was constructed to New Germantown, builders decided it would not be possible to tunnel through Conococheague Mountain so the venture was abandoned.

The Perry Lumber Company purchased a Climax locomotive in 1901 to remove 19,000 acres of timber from western Perry County. When the company disbanded in 1906, the track and land were sold to the Commonwealth, becoming one of the first large purchases for the Tuscarora State Forest.

Located in Tuscarora State Forest, this 10-mile trail was constructed in 1981 by the US Youth Conservation Corps, working with the Department of Environmental Resources' Bureau of Forestry.

Unlike some rail-trails, the Iron Horse Trail has some moderate climbs and requires good hiking boots. There are two different sections of the trail. The one on the north side of PA Route 274 follows the Path Valley Railroad grade; the one on the south side follows the Perry Lumber Company Railroad.

Big Spring State Park and its trailhead are located on PA274 near the Perry/Franklin County line. A second trailhead is located two miles southwest of New Germantown on Route 274.

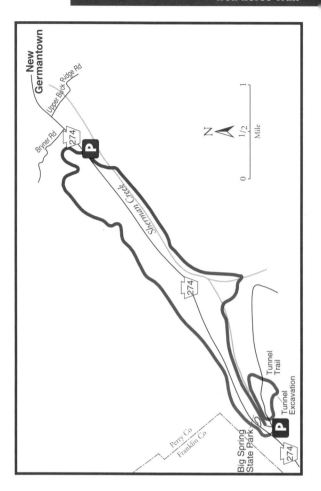

Location: Perry County
Miles: 10
Endpoints: Big Spring State Park to New Germantown
Surface: Dirt, original ballast
Contact: Bureau of Forestry
RD 1, Box 42A
Blain, PA 17006
717-536-3191

Ironton Rail-Trail

In 1882, the Ironton Railroad was purchased from the Lehigh Valley Railroad by the Thomas Iron Works Company to transport the tons of coal, iron ore, and limestone that fueled the nation's most powerful blast furnace. In that same year, David Thomas founded the village of Hokendauqua to house his employees. In 1996, Whitehall Township purchased the corridor from Conrail to create the Ironton Rail-Trail. The trail also traverses the Borough of Coplay and North Whitehall Township.

Boasting no fewer than 10 sites of historic significance, the former Ironton Railroad corridor is awash with the history of the Lehigh Valley. The trail cuts through the 110-acre Whitehall Parkway, preserving the remains of the limestone and cement industry that first brought wealth and recognition to the region. The corridor then splits as it approaches the Borough of Coplay, providing, when complete, a unique 6.25-mile loop through the Borough and the village of Hokendauqua along the Lehigh River, before rejoining the main corridor for the ride back to the village of Ironton. In Hokendauqua, the beautiful bridge over Lehigh Street is now finished with more improvements on the way.

The trail may be accessed at many points along its length. Parking is presently available in Whitehall Parkway. From Route 22E, take the exit for Route 145N (MacArthur Road). Follow MacArthur Road through several traffic lights to Chestnut Street. Turn left onto Chestnut Street and park behind the barn at Whitehall Parkway. The trail begins just down Chestnut Street from the parking lot.

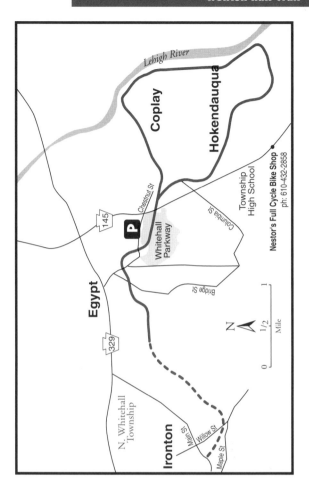

Location: Lehigh County
Miles: 9
Endpoints: Whitehall Township
Surface: Crushed stone and asphalt
Contact: Mary Ann Seagreaves
Whitehall Township
Bureau of Recreation
3219 MacArthur Road
Whitehall, PA 18052
610-437-5524

JFK Walking Trail

In 1925, the Pottsville Maroons football team brought great fame to Pottsville and Schuylkill County when it won the equivalent of today's Super Bowl after beating the Chicago Cardinals at Soldier Field.

Today Pottsville and Schuylkill County are again gaining fame but now the attraction is not football — it is trails. The 1.2 mile JFK Trail (pictured above) connects homes to recreation facilities and soon will be part of the Bartram Trail — which will one day stretch from Hamburg north to Minersville and possibly onward to Frackville. To the south of Pottsville near Berks County, a one-mile section of the Bartram Trail is now open with more miles to follow.

To access the JFK Walking Trail, travel Rt 61 north into Pottsville. Take a left at the light onto E. Norwegian St. Go right on Centre St. and left at the next light on Market St. (both PA 209) Make a right at the intersection of 12th and Market. Take a left at the stop sign on Laurel Blvd. Take a right at Laurel and 16th. Take the first left on York Farm Rd. to the JFK Recreation Complex.

Schuylkill Valley Heritage Trail

To the east of Pottsville, an eight-mile portion of the 16-mile Schuylkill Valley Heritage Trail (SVHT) is open. Running from Middleport to Tamaqua, the crushed stone surface connects the 1892 Tamaqua Railroad Station with the Newkirk Tunnel environmental education and historic recreation site.

While the section between Pottsville and Middleport is not complete, cyclist can still make the connection with Pottsville via Rt 209 — which offers good shoulders.

To access the SVHT from Pottsville, take 209 north through Middleport and continue towards Tamaqua. The trail borders PA 209. Park at the Newkirk Tunnel trailhead.

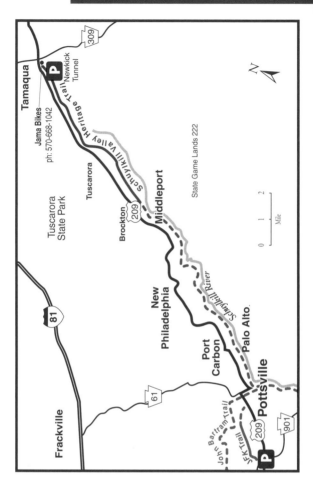

Location: Schuylkill County

Miles: 1.2 - JFK, 16 SVHT

Endpoints: Laurel Blvd. to York Farm Road

Surface: Asphalt - JFK, crushed stone - SVHT

Contact: "Porcupine Pat" McKinney
Schuylkill Conservation District
1206 Ag Center Drive
Pottsville, PA 17901
570-622-4124 x 113
570-622-4009
pmckinney@co.schuylkill.pa.us

Jim Mayer Riverswalk

The late Jim Mayer was a Johnstown area conservationist whose efforts to preserve natural resources have been incorporated into development of this trail. The land on which the trail is built was part of the Johnstown and Stonycreek Railroad. The Glosser Family Foundation subsequently bought the land from the former railroad and donated it to the Cambria County Transit Authority to be preserved. This 1.2-mile trail was dedicated on May 13, 1993 and provides recreation for local residents as well as travelers passing through the area.

The Jim Mayer Riverswalk Trail is nestled in the heart of Johnstown. As this beautiful trail winds along the Stonycreek River, it offers the tranquility of the Pennsylvania highlands amidst a metropolitan setting. The introduction of birdhouses along the trail has added to the existing natural habitat for wildlife, including deer.

To reach the trail, take PA403 (Central Avenue) in Johnstown south to Bridge Street in the Moxham District of the City. The trailhead is located on the left.

Another rail-trail nearby also offers visitors a path rich with history. The Allegheny Portage Railroad Trace follows the corridor of the Portage Railroad — which was built as the easiest means then available to connect the east and west sections of the Pennsylvania Canal. Passengers, freight and eventually whole canal boats were pulled by ropes on railroad cars over the Alleghenies on a series of ten steam-powered inclined planes. Although the Portage Railroad has been abandoned for almost a century and a half, many of its structures still stand.

The unique Skew Arch Bridge, built to carry a road over the Portage, is a marvel of well-preserved intricate stonework. Staple Bend Tunnel, the oldest railroad tunnel in the United States, survives on the western slope of the mountain near Johnstown and is slated for restoration.

To reach the Allegheny Portage Railroad Trace, take the Gallitzin Exit from Route 22 to the park's visitor center.

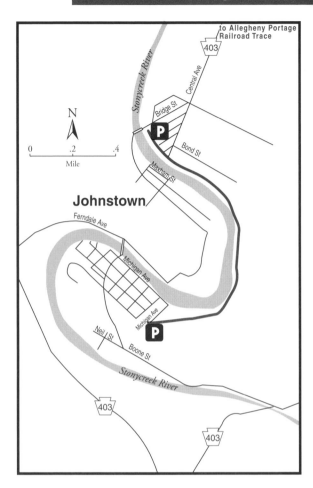

Location: Cambria County
Miles: 1.2
Endpoints: Moxham/Bridge Street to
Riverside/Michigan Avenue
(Johnstown)
Surface: Packed gravel
Contact: Rose Lucey-Noll
Cambria County Transit Authority
726 Central Avenue
Johnstown, PA 15902
814-535-5526

Kellettville to Nebraska Trace

Following the path of the long-abandoned Sheffield and Tionesta Railroad on the Tionesta Creek, the Kellettville to Nebraska Trace stretches from the US Army Corp of Engineers Kellettville Campground to the Nebraska Recreation Area. Initially constructed in the 1880s for lumber, freight, and occasional passenger service, the Sheffield and Tionesta was abandoned prior to its purchase by the US Forest Service in the 1930s. Currently the land which the trail traverses is administered by the Forest Service and the Corps of Engineers, but is maintained entirely by volunteer trail enthusiasts.

Most of the Kellettville to Nebraska Trace lies in and travels through a river environment. The primitive tread offers incredible scenery but with a price: users must cross four perennial streams without the aid of bridges. Chances to view wildlife are abound: turkey, grouse, whitetail deer, beaver, squirrel and black bear frequent the locale. Sharp-eyed hikers may spot hawks or even bald eagles!

To access the Kelletville to Nebraska trace, take Rt 62 north to Rt 666 to Kellettville. Trailhead parking is available at the Army Corps of Engineers Campground across the bridge from Rt 666.

For Nebraska Bridge trailhead access, follow Rt 36 south from Tionesta to Newmansville. Turn left and proceed four miles to the Nebraska Recreation Area.

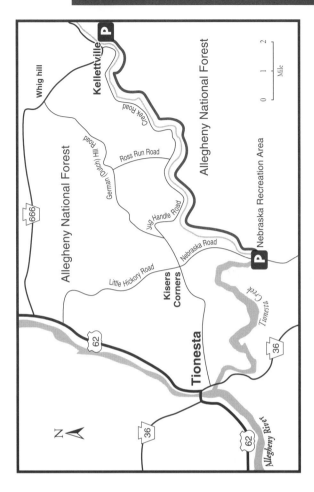

Location:	Forest County
Miles:	12.2
Endpoints:	Kellettville Campground to Nebraska Bridge Recreation Area
Surface:	Grass and dirt
Contact:	US Army Corps of Engineers
	One Tionesta Lake
	Tionesta, PA 16353
	814-755-3512

Kinzua Bridge Trail

The Kinzua railroad bridge was the highest railroad bridge in the world when it was built in 1882. Originally made of iron, the bridge is 301 feet high and spans the Kinzua Creek Valley for 2,053 feet. In 1890, the entire structure had to be rebuilt to accommodate heavier trains. It took more than 100 men working 10 hours a day exactly 105 days to complete a new 6.5 million pound steel structure. It is now the second highest railroad bridge in the country and the fourth highest in the world.

The Erie Railroad abandoned the bridge in 1959 and the line was sold for scrap to the Kovalchick Company, which then donated the bridge to the state. In 1970, the Kinzua State Park opened and in 1977 the Kinzua Bridge was placed on the National Register of Historic Civil Engineering Landmarks. Today, the Knox, Kane and Kinzua Railroad offers excursion rides over the bridge starting from Marienville or Kane.

Adventure awaits you on the Kinzua Bridge Trail. You'll follow the abandoned Erie Railroad line through a small portion of the 316-acre Kinzua Bridge State Park. After enjoying the woodlands and wildlife along the trail, you'll come to the highlight of your trip, the Kinzua railroad bridge. The faint of heart might want to stay on the overlook rather than walking out onto the bridge itself. For non-acrophobics, the bridge is equipped with a deck and railings so visitors can walk its full 2,053-foot length. You're guaranteed to be impressed by the scenery and amazing engineering of the second highest railroad bridge in the country.

Kinzua Bridge State Park is located 4 miles north of US Route 6 in Mt. Jewett on SR3011.

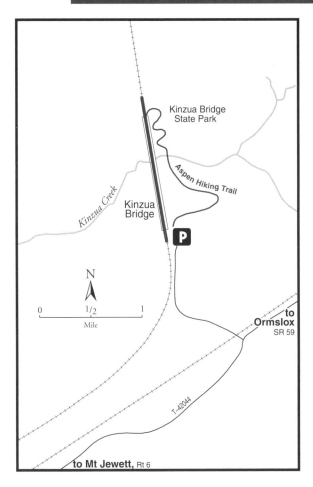

Location: McKean County
Miles: 1
Endpoints: Kinzua Bridge State Park
Surface: Wooden planks
Contact: Kinzua Bridge State Park
c/o Bendigo State Park
PO Box A
Johnsonburg, PA 15845
814-965-2646
www.dcnr.state.pa.us

Lackawanna River Heritage Trail

The Lackawanna River Heritage Trail is being developed by the Lackawana Heritage Valley Authority along 40 miles of the Lackawanna River located near Scranton, Pennsylvania. The trail follows abandoned sections of the Central Railroad of New Jersey and the former New York Ontario and Western Railway (NYO & W) between Scranton and Carbondale.

The Central New Jersey Rail Road (CNJRR) was part of the Lehigh Coal and Navigation system which operated the coal mine's railroads and canals to transport anthracite coal from the Lackawanna and Wyoming Valleys in Northeastern Pennsylvania to markets along the east coast. This portion of the CNJRR was abandoned after the flood of 1972. Additional sections of the Lackawanna River Heritage Trail are under development along the former New York Ontario and Western Railway (NYO & W) between Scranton and Carbondale. Several sections will open soon and will provide linkages to the D&H and O&W Trails.

A .5 mile section of trail runs adjacent to the Lackawanna River Corridor Association in North Scranton from West Market Street to Dean Street.

The 1.5 mile section of the LRHT runs from 7th Avenue to Elm Street in Scranton. There are three parking areas to access this trail; at 7th Avenue near Lackawanna Avenue, at the William Schmidt Recreation Park on Broadway Street and at Elm Street off South Washington Avenue. The three-mile section runs from David Masylar Park in Archbald on Laurel St. to Robert Mellow Park in Blakely on Keystone Ave. at River Street.

Currently, discontinuities exist even within the improved sections and road linkages are sometimes unclear. As a result, it is best to use a good local street map to make the various trail connections.

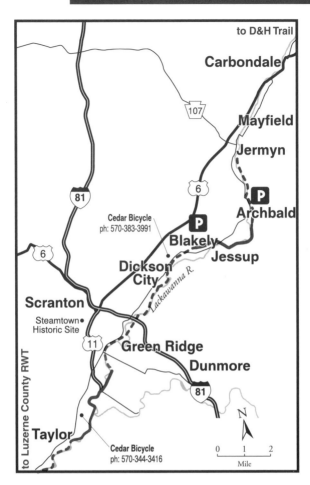

Location: Lackawanna County

Miles: 4.6 miles

Endpoints: North Seventh Avenue to Elm Street, City of Scranton, David Masylar Park to Robert Mellow Park

Surface: Crushed limestone on developed section. Dirt and cinder on other areas.

Contact: Lackawanna River Corridor Association
2006 North Main Avenue
Scranton, PA 18508
570-347-6311

Contact: Lackawanna Heritage Valley Authority
1300 Old Plank Road
Mayfield, PA 18433
570-876-6188

Lambs Creek Bike & Hike Trail

When the Tioga-Hammond Lakes were created by the US Army Corps of Engineers, the abandoned Erie Lackawanna Railroad became a trail.

Originally the Erie Railroad Tioga Division, the line once ran as far as Hoytville. It was abandoned after the Hurricane Agnes flood of 1972.

The Lambs Creek Recreation Area is situated next to Tioga Lakes and provides a variety of recreation opportunities. The 3.7 mile trail travels along the Tioga River, with fishing for tiger muskie, bass, walleye, and channel catfish among the pleasures to be found.

One other feature not to be missed is the overlook on the rock outcrops which separate Tioga and Hammond Lakes.

Take Lambs Creek Road just west of Mansfield on Route 6 to the trailhead in the park. The trail may also be accessed behind the BiLo Supermarket on North Main Street (Business US 15) in Mansfield.

Railroad Grade Trail

Originally built for the New York Central Railroad, this grade was relocated when the Tioga-Hammond Lakes were created by building the Tioga Dam and the Hammond Dam, two of 14 dams operated by the US Army Corps of Engineers (Baltimore District). The original railroad bed then became part of the Ives Run Recreation Area and opened in 1979.

A birdwatcher's delight, this leisurely trail is best explored with binoculars. With Crooked Creek on your right and state game lands on your left, you'll observe a variety of songbirds, waterfowl, and gamebirds as you travel through the Bryant Hollow Wildlife Management Area. The trail is closed April to August for Osprey Breeding and open to automobiles from October through December.

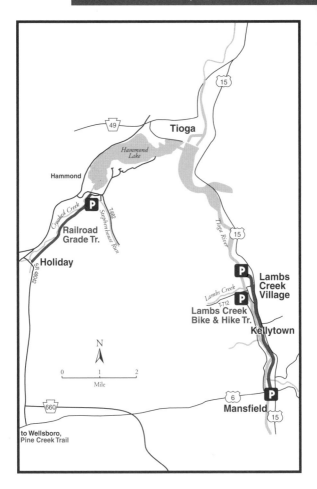

Location: Tioga County
Miles: 3.7 - Lambs Cr, 2.6 - Railroad Grade
Endpoints: Lambs Creek Recreation Area
to Mansfield,
Ives Run Recreation Area to Holiday
Surface: Asphalt
Contact: US Army Corps of Engineers
RR 1, Box 65
Tioga, PA 16946-9733
570-835-5281

Lancaster Junction Trail

Originally the Reading & Columbia Railroad, this branch of the Reading Railroad was built to haul anthracite coal to Columbia where it was loaded into barges on the Susquehanna and Tidewater Canal for shipment to the port of Baltimore. The Reading also owned the canal and used it to compete directly with rival Pennsylvania Railroad for Baltimore coal traffic. After the canal ceased operation in 1894, the railroad became just another rural branch line. It was abandoned in 1985 and became a trail in 1987.

The Lancaster Junction Trail travels through meadows, past rich Lancaster farmland and along winding Chickies Creek. This trail is perfect for horseback riding, cross-country skiing, or jogging.

The southern trailhead near Landisville is found at the end of Champ Boulevard, just east of Spooky Nook Road and the Salunga exit of I-283. The trail may also be accessed just west of Lancaster Junction on Auction Road.

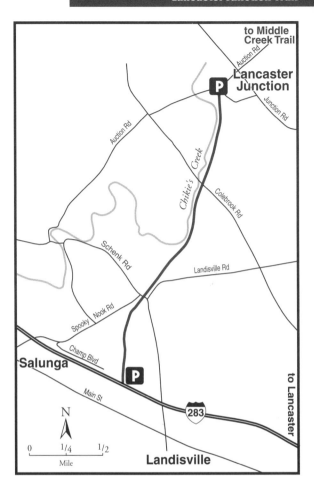

Location:	Lancaster County
Miles:	2.3
Endpoints:	Lancaster Junction to Landisville
Surface:	Cinder
Contact:	Lancaster County Parks & Recreation
	1052 Rockford Road
	Lancaster, PA 17602
	717-295-3605

Lebanon Valley Rail-Trail

Created from the former Cornwall-Lebanon Railroad built by Robert H. Coleman in the 1880s, the Lebanon Valley Rail-Trail follows a route rich with social and economic history. In the old days, special passenger trains carried visitors to the popular summer resort community of Mt. Gretna. During the 1800s and early 1900s, the railroad also provided transport to the Pennsylvania National Guard training encampment near Mt. Gretna. Eventually passenger service ceased, and the Pennsylvania Railroad acquired the line. Freight service to the main line in Lancaster County continued until Hurricane Agnes washed out sections of track in 1972. In 1999 Lebanon Valley Rails-to-Trails acquired the corridor to develop a multi-use trail.

The recently completed first phase of the trail offers a relaxing tour through the woodlands of southern Lebanon County. Beginning in the community of Colebrook, the trail follows a gentle grade through the hills of Mt. Gretna skirting the boundaries of State Game Lands 145 and Governor Dick Recreation Area. Just east of Colebrook, trail users can find a nice view of Lake Duffy — a former ice dam now partially drained and home to a variety of waterfowl and other wildlife. More adventurous visitors may choose to explore a connecting hiking trail to the observation tower on Governor Dick Hill; the sight of the Lebanon County countryside is spectacular!

One note: the trail is adjacent to gamelands so do be mindful of hunting seasons.

By summer 2002, the links from Colebrook to the Conewago Trail and from Cornwall to Zinns Mill Rd. should be complete — which will bring the total mileage up to 11.5!

To access the Lebanon Valley Rail-Trail in Colebrook, take the Pennsylvania Turnpike to the Mt. Gretna interchange — Exit 20. Follow Rt. 72 north to Rt. 117. Follow Rt. 117 north about five miles to the Colebrook trailhead. Park at the trailhead at the intersection of Rt. 117 and Colebrook Rd.

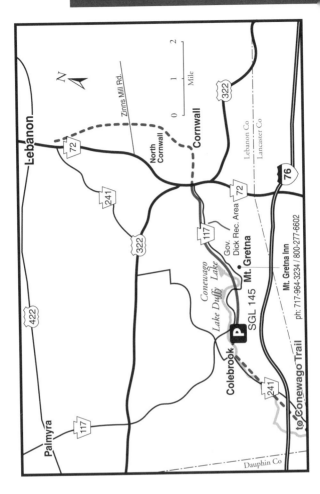

 on parallel wood-chip trail

Location: Lebanon County
Miles: 5
Endpoints: Colebrook to Route 72
Surface: Crushed Limestone
Contact: John B. Wengert
Lebanon Valley Rails-to-Trails
P.O. Box 2043
Cleona, PA 17042
717-867-2101
jbweng@aol.com

Lehigh Canal (North)

Josiah White built the Lehigh Canal to transport the recently discovered anthracite coal from Mauch Chunk (now Jim Thorpe) to Easton, PA. There boats entered the Delaware Canal to complete their journey to Philadelphia. Others proceeded eastward along the Morris Canal to New York City.

The Lehigh Canal was 46 miles long and used 44 locks and 8 dams to conquer the 364 foot elevation change (see locks on map). The locks were constructed to be 100 feet and 22 feet wide allowing two boats to pass at once. The dams ranged in depth from eight to twenty feet. Remnants of these locks and dams, as well as the historic buildings can still be seen from the towpath.

Today, the canal is part of a larger national park known as the National Heritage Corridor. Located near the Lehigh Gorge State Park Trail and the Switchback Rail-Trail, the Carbon County section of the towpath is approximately six miles long. It is a popular place to hike, bicycle, cross country ski, ice skate, and fish. In addition, new trails are maintained along a wooded section of the trail which leads to more remote accesses of the Lehigh River. Wildlife such as beaver, mink, deer, and water fowl are common sights along the banks of the canal and river.

Easy access to the park can be found in the community of Weissport. To get there from Interstate 476 (PA Turnpike Northeast Extension) Exit 74, take 209 south to the traffic light. Turn right onto Canal Street. Make a left at the stop sign and an immediate right into the public parking lot. From Route 248, continue straight across the intersection when you have come to the end of the highway. Make a left at the stop sign and an immediate right into the public parking lot. The trail proceeds north to Jim Thorpe or south (across the street) to Parryville.

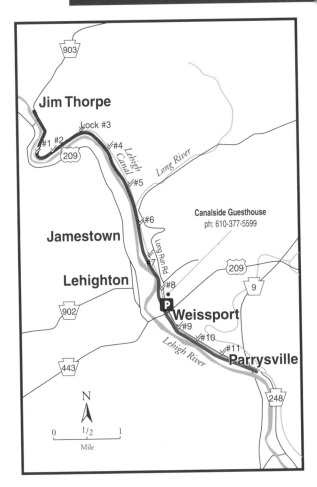

Location: Carbon County
Miles: 5.5
Endpoints: Parryville, Jim Thorpe
Surface: Crushed stone, dirt
Contact: Christina van Gelder
Lehigh Canal Recreation Commission
P.O. Box 85
Ashfield, PA 18212
610-377-3856

Lehigh Canal (South)

As a segment of the Delaware and Lehigh Canal National Heritage Corridor, the Lehigh Canal represents the evolution of both systematic canal transportation and natural resource conservation. The Corridor and its people made outstanding contributions to our nations social and industrial growth from 1682 on, and particularly between 1817 and 1930. Today the Corridor represents a living "national park" where people work, play and live.

The 17 mile segment between Allentown and Easton offers a look into both the past and the future. During colonial times, the Liberty Bell rested secretly in Allentown — protected from destruction by the English. And Easton hosted one of only three public readings of the Declaration of Independence. In the future, additional segments along the Delaware and Lehigh National Heritage Corridor will be linked through the conservation and natural resource development efforts to produce 150 mile of trail from Wilkes-Barre south to Bristol.

To access the trail in Allentown, take US 22 east towards New Jersey. In Allentown, get off on the exit for Airport Road. Follow Airport Road south approximately two miles, until it becomes Irving Street. Follow Irving Street 1.25 miles to Hanover Avenue. Go right on Hanover, which will turn into Hamilton and take a left on Fullerton Avenue. Make a right and cross the river over a small bridge in West Catasauqua, and go right on Dauphin Street. Cross over the lock and make a left into Lehigh Canal Park.

To access Hugh Moore Park from U.S. 22 take 25th Street South (1.6 miles) to Lehigh Drive, turn right and go .5 mile to stop sign. Turn right and cross the old green Glendon Bridge. Then go right and follow the signs to the trailhead/picnic area.

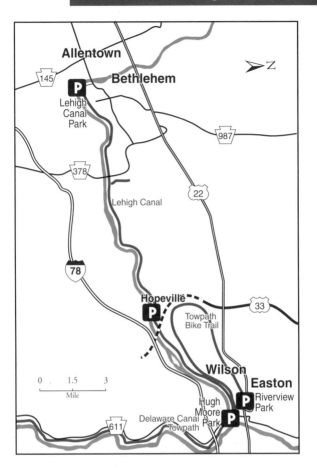

Location:	Northampton County
Miles:	17
Endpoints:	Allentown to Easton
Surface:	Crushed stone, dirt
Contact:	D & L National Heritage Corridor
	10 East Church Street
	Bethlehem, PA 18018
	610-861-9345

Lehigh Gorge State Park Trail

This trail is located in the Lehigh Gorge State Park, an area best known for its whitewater rafting.

The trail was built along a rail line that was originally constructed by the Central Railroad of New Jersey. The line traversed the Lehigh Gorge to tap the anthracite coal fields in the Hazleton and Wilkes-Barre areas. With coal exhausted, other business could not sustain the Central Railroad, which made way for the Lehigh Valley Railroad in 1965. The Lehigh Valley Railroad then abandoned the line in 1972.

North of Jim Thorpe, the right-of-way parallels an active Conrail track for six miles. This rails-with-trails option is one of 61 similar joint-use ventures in the nation. The active track is used six to eight times daily; the trail accommodates approximately 30,000 trail users each year. There have never been any trail-track related accidents.

Spectacular scenery and roaring rapids await you in the Lehigh Gorge. Remember to bring your camera for this trail! You'll click the shutter more than a few times as you follow the Lehigh River along its rocky escarpments. If you would like to experience the river in a more personal way, there are also many opportunities for kayaking, canoeing, rafting, and fishing.

To reach the northern trailhead near White Haven, take Exit 273 from I-80 into White Haven Borough. The southern trailhead just outside of Jim Thorpe is located on Coalport Road, just north of PA903 in Jim Thorpe. To reach Jim Thorpe from I-476, the Pennsylvania Turnpike Northeast Extension, take Exit 74 towards Jim Thorpe.

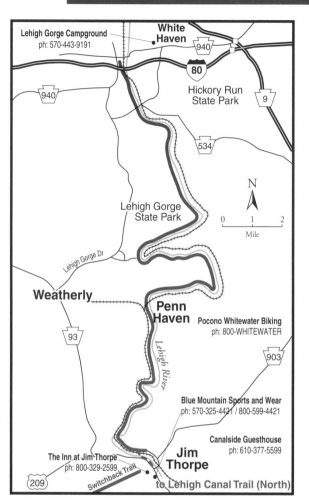

 on certain sections

Location: Luzerne and Carbon Counties
Miles: 25
Endpoints: White Haven to Jim Thorpe
Surface: Cinder, crushed stone
Contact: Lehigh Gorge State Park
c/o Hickory Run State Park
RR 1, Box 81
White Haven, PA 18661
570-443-0400
www.dcnr.state.pa.us

LeTort Spring Run Nature Trail

James LeTort, the namesake for the stream and trail, was a noted pioneer who lived near the banks of LeTort Spring Run. Mr. LeTort acted as interpreter for the government when communicating with local Native Americans.

The South Mountain Iron Company built the railroad around 1870 to run from Carlisle along LeTort Spring Run to Pine Grove Furnace. After 1891, the Reading Railroad operated the line until the Hurricane Agnes flood in 1972. The LeTort Regional Authority purchased the right-of-way in 1974 and converted it into a 1.4-mile nature trail.

Surrounding the trail is a mixture of deciduous trees, including oak, maple, and locust. Along the banks of the LeTort are many lowland marshes with cattails, marsh grasses, and a variety of animals, including muskrats, ducks, salamanders, and frogs.

Easiest access to the trail is found in LeTort Park, on East Pomfret Street in the Borough of Carlisle. From High Street, turn south on Spring Garden, then west onto Pomfret Street. The park is on the left. A second trailhead is located on Bonnybrook Road, just east of Route 34. Going south on Route 34, Lindsay Lane is a left turn, .7 miles past Exit 47 of I-81. Bonnybrook Road intersects with Lindsay Lane.

Please note the trail diverges from the corridor just after the railroad bridge in Letort Park. The detour cuts through the forest and through an apartment complex parking lot, and follows Bedford Street south — or left — to a dead end at the school. The trail hops back on to the rail bed across the grassy field to the left of the path to the school.

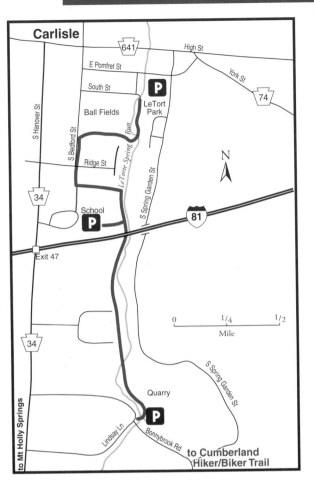

Location: Cumberland County

Miles: 1.4

Endpoints: Carlisle to South Middleton Township

Surface: Original ballast

Contact: Brian Fischbach
LeTort Regional Authority
415 Franklin Street
Carlisle, PA 17013
717-245-0508

Lititz/Warwick Trailway

The Lititz / Warwick Trailway is a remnant of the Reading Railroad, also known as the Reading Company. The Company was established to haul anthracite coal in 1883. Company business boomed, and Reading Company lines stretched into Delaware and New Jersey. By the late 1800s, the Reading Company was the largest corporation in the world's largest industrial region.

As the 1800s drew to a close, the Reading Company was ruled a monopoly and suffered fragmentation. During the early to mid 1900s, the coal industry declined at an increasing rate. By 1971, the company could no longer afford to operate.

The Lititz / Warwick Trailway traverses developed and agricultural land both in the Township and the Borough of Lititz. The trail serves the walking, jogging, biking, and cross-country skiing needs of the community. Linking the Bonfield Elementary School, Lititz Run Creek Greenway, and the Township Municipal Campus, the trail provides a connection for residents of nearby developments with schools, workplaces, recreational opportunities, and more. This trail provides a corridor for residents to the Linear Park that extends from Lititz to Warwick Township. In the future, the trail will serve as a foundation for further development of a regional trail network.

To access the Lititz / Warwick Trailway, follow 501 north from Lancaster to 772. Follow 772 east to Clay Road. Turn left on Clay Road and continue to the Warwick Municipal Campus.

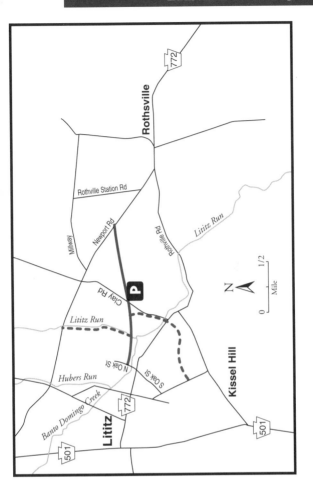

Location: Lancaster County
Miles: 1.4, .6 miles improved
Endpoints: Oak St., Lititz to Newport Road, Warwick
Surface: Asphalt
Contact: Dan Zimmerman
Warwick Township
P.O. Box 308
Lititz, PA 17543
717-626-8900

Little Buffalo State Park Trail

The Little Buffalo State Park Trail is located in Little Buffalo State Park in Perry County. This trail has connections to 7 miles of hiking trails located within the State Park. Highlights alongside the trail include access to fishing along Holman Lake, a covered bridge over Furnace Run, Shoaff's Grist Mill, and an original rail car "Way Car No. 12."

The Newport and Shermans Valley Railroad traversed Perry County hauling lumber, tan bark, freight, and passengers. The construction of the first 16 miles of the steam powered railroad only took about 6 months in 1890 at the cost of $7,900 per mile. By 1893, the Newport and Shermans Valley Railroad traveled another 14 miles from Loysville to New Germantown.

In 1913, it only cost 72 cents to ship 480 pounds of freight 25 miles from Newport to Blain. The Newport and Shermans Valley Railroad transported vital deliveries of tan bark to tanneries in Newport. Also it was a popular passenger train with each town along the track having its own train station. The railway was last used in the early 1930s, when it succumbed to financial difficulties and changing times.

Little Buffalo State Park is comprised of 830 acres in scenic Perry County. Travel PA Route 34 and exit west between New Bloomfield and Newport. The rail-trail can be accessed at Shoaff's Mill and the Main Picnicking Area end of Little Buffalo State Park. Parking is available at both locations.

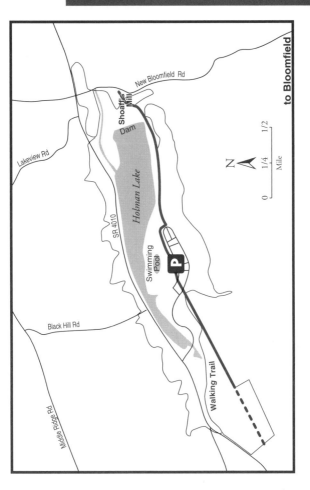

Location: Perry County
Miles: 2.5 miles
Endpoints: Shoaff's Mill to the Western Border of Little Buffalo State Park
Surface: Dirt/Gravel
Contact: Little Buffalo State Park
  RD 2 Box 256A
  Newport, PA 17074-9428
  717-567-9255
  www.dcnr.state.pa.us

Lower Trail

Follow the Path of Progress from Canal, to Rail, to Trail. The Lower (rhymes with "flower") Trail follows the corridor of the old Pennsylvania Canal. Built in the 1830s, the canal was a continuous system of waterways and railroads from Philadelphia to Pittsburgh.

As improvements were made to locomotives, the "iron horse" soon proved superior to mule-towed canal boats, and by the 1850s the Pennsylvania Railroad had replaced the slow and inefficient canal system.

In 1879, a railroad known as the Petersburg Branch was built along the corridor and continued to operate until 1979. In 1990, the line was purchased by the local rails-to-trails group with a donation made by Attorney T.Dean Lower.

Following the Frankstown Branch of the Juniata River, the Lower Trail features beautiful scenery through forest and farmland as well as portions of canal locks, channels and lock tender house remnants. The trail also passes the Mt. Etna Furnace, where iron ore was smelted.

From Hollidaysburg, travel east on US22, 9 miles to PA Route 866. At the bottom of Short Mountain, turn right on PA SR 866 and proceed into Williamsburg, where 866 becomes First Street. Stay on First Street past Martin General Store, go two blocks farther to trailhead parking just past Past-to-Present Cafe / Bicycle Rentals at the intersection of First and Liberty Streets. For Alexandria, follow US22 18.5 miles east from Hollidaysburg. Pass the Waterstreet Flea Market on the right and then, just before the bridge over the river, turn left on SR4014 toward Alexandria. Go .4 miles to trailhead parking.

A 5.25 mile trail extension from Williamsburg westward to Flowing Springs is under construction and will be completed by fall 2002. To access the new tread, follow US22 east 8.2 miles past Canoe Creek State Park to Flowing Spring Road. Turn right and continue 1 mile to trailhead parking. Also, in conjunction with upgrades to US22, a link connecting the trail to Canoe Creek State Park will be completed by 2004.

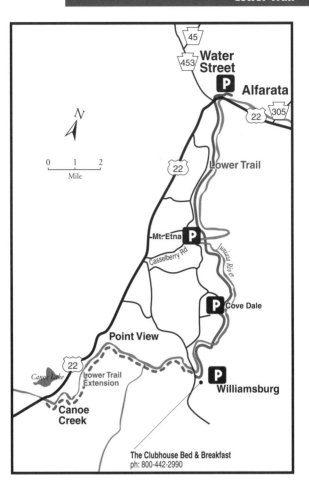

Location:	Blair and Huntingdon Counties
Miles:	11
Endpoints:	Alexandria to Williamsburg
Surface:	Crushed limestone
Contact:	Jennifer Barefoot
	Rails-to-Trails of Central Pennsylvania
	PO Box 529
	Hollidaysburg, PA 16648
	814-832-2400

Luzerne County Rail-Trail

During the mid 1800's the heavy demand for anthracite coal spurred development of many small urban communities in the Lackawanna and Wyoming Valleys. An extensive infrastructure of railroads hauled the coal away from the mines of northeast Pennsylvania to fuel the industrial revolution.

Today the Lackawanna and Wyoming Valleys are producing rail-trails to fuel a trails and greenways revolution. With existing trails like the Lehigh Gorge State Park Trail and the Back Mountain Trail and proposed trails like the Hazleton Area Rail-Trail and the Susquehanna Warrior Trail, the region hopes to link together its tremendous wealth of natural resources with a network of trails.

A two-mile segment of the Luzerne County Rail-Trail is open with continued development in the works. Connecting with not only the boroughs between Old Forge and Wilkes-Barre, but also the nearby trails, such as the Lackawanna River Heritage Trail, the Luzerne County Rail-Trail will be a major regional asset.

The Luzerne County Rail-Trail is a rail-with-trail — the trail shares right-of-way with an active rail line. Rail-with-trails have become quite popular with nine other such facilities in Pennsylvania and a total of 61 rail-with-trails across the nation. Recent detailed research from RTC suggests rail-with-trails to offer communities both safe and enjoyable recreation and transportation.

To access the Luzerne County Rail-Trail in Pittston, travel I-81 north from Hazleton about 30 miles. Take Exit 175A towards Pittston and merge on to Rt. 315 N. Travel 1.4 miles and turn left on Rt. 2035. Next take a slight left to merge on to US 11. Travel on US 11 to N. Main Street and turn left. A quick right on Water Street followed by a quick left on Kennedy Blvd leads to the trailhead at the park.

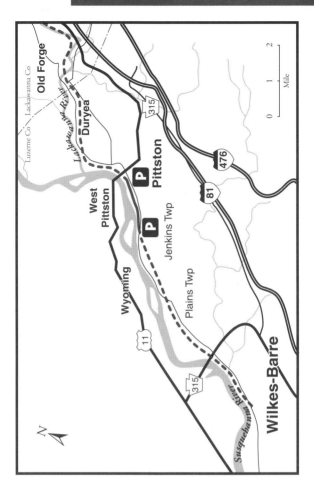

Location: Luzerne and Lackawanna Counties
Miles: 11.6, 1.8 open
Endpoints: Old Forge to Wilkes-Barre
Surface: Crushed stone
Contact: John Charles
Luzerne County Parks Department
2000 Wyoming Avenue
Forty Fort, PA 18704
570-331-7046

Lycoming Creek Bikeway

Named "Legani Hanne" or "sandy creek" by the Delaware tribe, Lycoming Creek and its adjacent rail corridor have a significant history. Hundreds of years ago, these Native Americans developed a long foot trail along Lycoming Creek, which was known first as the Sheseguin Trail and later as Culbertson's Path. This trail spanned from Onondago, New York to the Carolinas.

In 1839, the first railroad in Lycoming County was constructed along a portion of the trail from Williamsport to Ralston. The railroad was later extended to Elmira, New York. The railroad and creek were heavily used to transport iron ore, coal and lumber from mines, grist mills and sawmills north of Williamsport, which was the lumber capital of the world in the late 19th century. The railroad even transported Confederate prisoners to a Union camp in Elmira during the Civil War.

Shortly after the Hurricane Agnes flood of 1972, the Penn Central Railroad Elmira Branch was abandoned by Conrail. The current bikeway was built in 1991 along sections of this historic corridor, and also shares several well-marked streets in a residential area.

Following Lycoming Creek, and providing connections to the 11-mile bikeway system in the Williamsport Urbanized Area, the trail passes Carl E. Stotz Memorial Park with its monument to Mr. Stotz, the founder of Little League Baseball. Eventually the trail comes to a wooden pedestrian bridge crossing Lycoming Creek. The journey ends about a mile later at the Heshbon Recreation Park. Local efforts to continue the bikeway northward along the railroad are underway.

To access the trail from Williamsport, take Lycoming Creek Road north and take a left on Heshbon Road just before crossing the river. Continue .5 miles to Heshbon Park and parking.

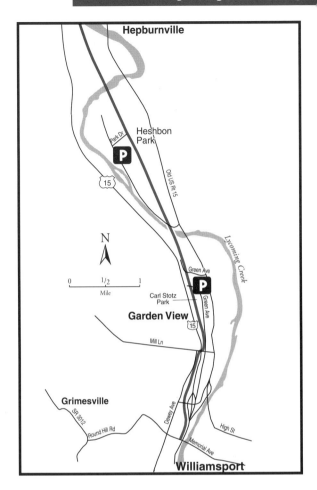

Location: Lycoming County
Miles: 5.5
Endpoints: Hepburnville to Memorial Avenue, Williamsport
Surface: Asphalt
Contact: Mark Murawski
Lycoming County Planning Commission
48 West Third Street
Williamsport, PA 17701
570-320-2138

Mahoning Shadow Trail

The Mahoning Shadow Trail stretches 15 miles along the corridor of the former Penn Central Railroad. At its terminus in Fordham, the trail winds along the scenic Mahoning Creek and passes several coke ovens. Within the borough of Punxsutawney — home of the world famous groundhog Punxsutawney Phil — the trail diverges from the Penn Central corridor and the Mahoning Creek. Rejoining the Mahoning Creek on the eastern side of the Borough, the trail passes Cloe and climbs above the creek bed to the scenic highlands near its eastern terminus at the village of Hudson.

During the summer of 2000, the Punxsutawney Area Rails-to-Trails Association renovated the trestle crossing the Mahoning Creek. A combination of grant funding and volunteer labor provided the resources to link the Borough with points east. During the upcoming summer of 2001, the trail will gain a crushed limestone surface between Punxsutawney and Fordham.

Currently, the Mahoning Shadow Trail offers an enjoyable yet unimproved surface with little signage. Spring 2002 construction, though will provide the segment between Punxsuatawny and Fordham with a fresh surface of crushed stone.

To access the trail in Punxsutawney, travel Route 119 N about 30 miles from Indiana. Once within the limits of Punxsutawney, pass Indiana and Spruce Streets on the right. Turn left by Joe's Drive-in and park in the ballfield lot. If you pass McCabe's Funeral Home, you passed the turnoff to the ballfield lot.

No visit to Punxsutawney would be complete without a visit with Punxsutawney Phil — the famous groundhog with a knack for forecasting the arrival of spring. Contact the Chamber of Commerce to locate Phil or to learn more about Groundhog Day festivities.

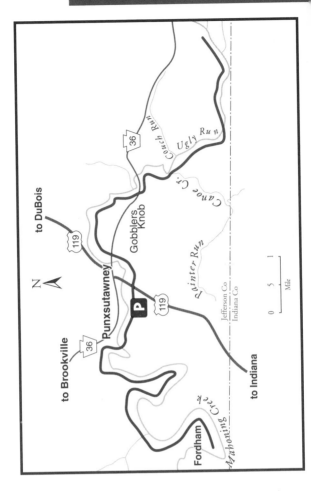

Location: Jefferson County
Miles: 15
Endpoints: Fordham to Hudson
Surface: Unimproved
Contact: Rodney Rhodes
Jefferson County Department of Development
155 Main Street, Second Floor
Brookeville, PA 15825
814-849-3047

Middle Creek Trail

In June 1914, the Ephrata and Lebanon Street Railway Company completed construction of a 22.7-mile trolley line between the towns of Ephrata and Lebanon. Passing through the nine small towns, the trip took an hour and a half.

All that remains of the line is the one-mile Middle Creek Trail, located on State Game Lands 46 in Lancaster County. Acting as the eastern side of a triangle formed with the Elders Run Trail and the 130-mile Horseshoe Trail, the Middle Creek Trail is contained within the Middle Creek Wildlife Management Area.

Encompassing 5,000 acres of protected habitat, the Management Area is seasonal home to thousands of migrating ducks, swans, and Canada Geese, as well as the year-round host to a bevy of pheasant, quail, ruffed grouse, and deer. Middle Creek also offers an informative visitors center and interpretive trails, including a Braille trail for the visually impaired.

To reach Middle Creek, take I-78 to Exit 13 and proceed south on PA501 to Schaefferstown. Go east on Route 897 to Kleinfeltersville. Turn right on Hopeland Road to the Wildlife Management Area. To hike a downhill return trip, continue on Hopeland Road to Mountain Spring Road and turn right. Park in lot for State Gamelands on the right; follow Elders Run Trail a few hundred feet to Middle Creek Trail.

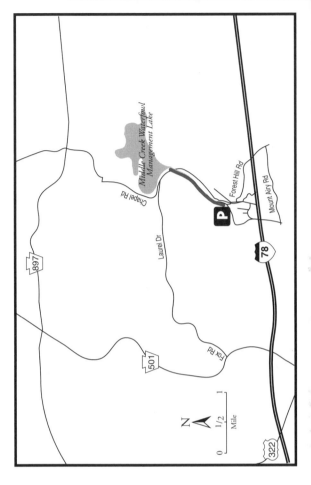

Location: Lancaster County
Miles: 1
Endpoints: Within management area
Surface: Dirt, grass
Contact: Middle Creek Wildlife
Management Area
PO Box 820
Newmanstown, PA 17073
717-733-1512

Montour Trail

The Montour Railroad was built between 1877 and 1914 — linking the Pittsburgh and Lake Erie Railroad with more than 30 coal mines. Forming a semi-circle around the city of Pittsburgh, the Montour also connected other railroads, including the Pennsylvania, the Pittsburgh & West Virginia, the Baltimore & Ohio, and the Union.

When completed, the Montour Trail's 55 miles will connect the Ohio and Monongahela Rivers, crossing numerous creeks and highways on a variety of bridges, including one almost 1,000 feet long, and three tunnels.

The main historical feature on the Cecil segment of the trail is the 620-foot National Tunnel, which passes under Klinger Road. This unusual tunnel is built on a curve and you will not be able to see one portal while standing at the other.

In winter, locals refer to this as the "National Cave" because of the icy stalactites that form in the tunnel. Many of these icicles reach halfway to the tunnel floor! Because of this phenomenon, the trail in the tunnel is surfaced with a coarse aggregate stone, which allows water to pass easily through to the french drains along the south side of the tunnel.

On the eastern end, take I-79 Exit 48 — the Southpointe exit. Follow signs to Hendersonville (about one mile). Turn left just past Hendersonville Post Office, go up hill about 100 yards and turn right into trailhead.

The northernmost point on the Montour Trail is located in the community of Groveton. It is accessed from I-79 by taking Exit 64 — the Coraopolis exit, proceeding west on Route 51 about 0.3 miles. Immediately after crossing a bridge, switchback right onto Montour Road. Returning east about 0.1 miles, and park at the trailhead under the bridge.

To reach the Cecil segment, take Route 50 west from I-79 at Exit 54 — the Bridgeville exit. About three miles west of the end of the four lane portion of Rt 50, Cecil Twp Park is on the left. Park in western lot (near municipal building) and follow signs across the creek and up access trail.

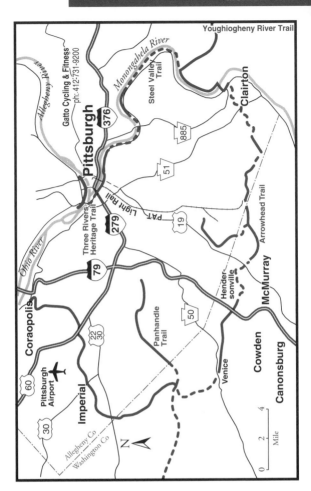

 on certain sections

Location:	Washington and Allegheny Counties
Miles:	Five segments of 17.5, 4.5, 3.7, 2.1, and 1.5
Endpoints:	Coraopolis (Groveton) to Quicksilver;
	Venice (Cecil Park) to Hendersonville;
	Rt 19 to Brush Run Road;
	Logan Road to county line;
	Triphammer Rd to Stewart Road
Surface:	Crushed limestone
Contact:	Montour Trail Council
	PO Box 11866
	Pittsburgh, PA 15228-0866
	412-831-2030
	www.montourtrail.org

Nor-Bath Trail

For 77 years, the tiny Northampton & Bath Railroad traveled the seven miles between the two towns which gave the line its name. Located in the heart of Northampton County's cement district, the N&B's trains supplied its larger cousins, the Central of New Jersey, Lehigh & New England, and Delaware, Lackawanna & Western, with cement, bringing in limestone, gypsum and coal to US Steel and its successors. Perhaps its most famous contribution to railroad history is its place as the first US railroad to become completely dieselized.

Like its larger cousins, the N&B fell victim to the changing face of transportation and the rise of the trucking industry. Abandoned in 1979, the corridor's purchase by Northampton County's Park Board allows the "little train that could" to continue to serve its namesake towns by connecting their parks (Bicentennial and Jacksonville, as well as a proposed regional park), schools (George Wolf and Jacksonville) and historic centers (Franklin Fort and the Craig settlement, the county's earliest Scotch-Irish community). Plans to expand the trail into both Northampton and Bath are on the county's drawing board.

To reach the trail at Jacksonville Park, take Route 512 south from Bath and turn right after two miles onto Jacksonville Road. The park is just ahead on the right and the trailhead is a few hundred feet ahead on the left.

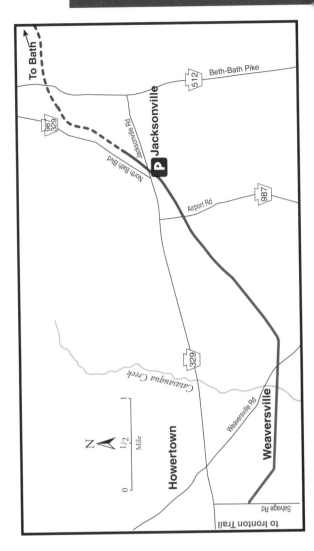

Location:	Northampton County
Miles:	5.2, 3.8 improved
Endpoints:	Weaversville to Jacksonville
Surface:	Dirt, crushed stone
Contact:	Northampton County
	Parks & Recreation
	RD 4, Greystone Building
	Nazareth, PA 18064-9278
	610-746-1975

O & W Trail

Built in the 1880s to transport coal mined from the Lackawanna Valley's rich anthracite deposits, the New York, Ontario & Western's Scranton Division was just one part of a network of rails and canals connecting the Wyoming Valley to the East Coast.

By the 1940s, the demand for anthracite coal had declined, and the rails that once transported this vital energy source were slowly abandoned. When it was abandoned in 1957, the NYO&W was the largest railroad to be abandoned in the United States.

Along the trail, you will see beautiful views of the upper Lackawanna River, Shehawken Creek, Stillwater Cliffs, Stillwater Reservoir, and Stoneface. There are also lakes, wetlands, woodlands, and small communities that offer a variety of recreational activities.

The Delaware & Hudson (D&H) Trail (see page 42) parallels the O&W Rail-Trail for much of its length. The Rail-Trail Council of Northeastern Pennsylvania will be developing the D&H, using the O&W for loop trails, but with little improvements other than grading.

To reach Simpson, take I-81 to Exit 191A, and then Route 6 to Carbondale. After the town of Carbondale, turn left onto Route 171. Continue about one mile, park on right side of viaduct in Simpson. Enter the O&W along Homestead Street.

The northern 13 miles of the trail to the Delaware River is owned by Preston and Buckingham Townships. To access this section of the trail, take PA370 to Lakewood. The corridor is readily apparent, at the train station in the center of town.

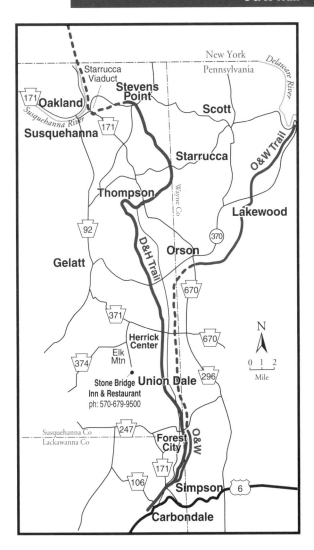

Location:	Lackawanna, Wayne and Susquehanna Co.
Miles:	13 completed, 8 planned
Endpoints:	Simpson to Stillwater
Surface:	Cinder, original ballast
Contact:	Lynn Conrad
	Rail-Trail Council of NE Pennsylvania
	PO Box 123
	Forest City, PA 18421-0123
	570-785-7245

115

Oil Creek State Park Trail

The Titusville and Petroleum Center Railroad had one major purpose when it was built in 1863—to transport oil. Oil was discovered in Oil Creek Valley in 1859 by Colonel Edward Drake and William Smith. Almost overnight, towns such as Titusville, Miller Farm, Pioneer, and Petroleum Center blossomed as opportunists rushed to get rich from the "Great Oil Dorado."

The oil boom ended in 1871 almost as quickly as it began. When the once-boisterous towns died, the railroad hung on. Through a series of mergers, it became part of the Pennsylvania Railroad system in 1900 and was abandoned in 1945.

Few reminders of the thousands of people who once occupied the Oil Creek Valley remain. Today, the valley is home to hemlocks, beaver ponds, trout streams and waterfalls. The only evidence of the intense oil drilling that once went on here is the occasional well head.

Oil Creek State Park has 36 miles of hiking trails with camping shelters; 20 miles of cross-country ski trails; picnicking, canoeing, fishing, and bicycle rentals. The Oil Creek & Titusville excursion train runs through the park.

For the south trailhead, take the Route 8 bypass north around Oil City and continue 3 miles and turn towards Petroleum Center on SR1007 just after Route 8 crosses Oil Creek. Continue 3 miles to the junction of SR1007 and SR1004. Turn right on SR1004 and cross Oil Creek. Parking is .1 miles ahead on the left.

For the northern trailhead at Drake Well Museum, again take the Route 8 bypass around Oil City, and proceed 14.0 miles north back to Route 8. Continue .4 miles and take a right at the light on Bloss Street. If you reach the junction with Route 27 you have passed Bloss Street. Continue just over .75 miles to trailhead parking on the right before the bridge.

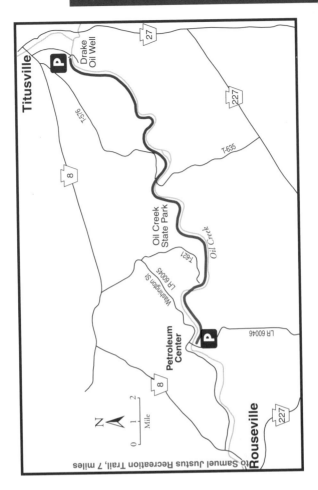

Location: Venango County

Miles: 9.7

Endpoints: Petroleum Center to
Drake Well Museum

Surface: Asphalt

Contact: Oil Creek State Park
RR 1, Box 207
Oil City, PA 16301
814-676-5915
www.dcnr.state.pa.us

Panhandle Trail

The Conrail line once known as the Panhandle Railroad was a vital link that connected Pittsburgh to Cincinnati, Chicago and St. Louis. Today, this corridor is undergoing a metamorphosis into a multi-use, non-motorized trail that will link Washington County with points west such as Weirton, WV, Pittsburgh, Washington DC, and beyond.

The Washington County Segment is approximately 17.3 miles long and passes through nine municipalities, providing much-needed recreational and health facilities to a mostly rural population, improving quality of life for citizens of all ages.

Officially dedicated as Washington County's 4th park, the Panhandle Trail is now recognized as a valuable resource and landmark for residents of Pennsylvania, becoming the Commonwealth's 100th successful rail-trail project. Officials of Washington County, along with officials from Allegheny County, the West Virginia Rail Authority, PennDOT, the United States Surface Transportation Board, the PA DCNR, and the Southwestern Pennsylvania Commission, continue to work to preserve the historic corridor.

To access the Panhandle Trail (as well as the Montour Trail) near the village of Primrose, follow 22W from Pittsburgh to 980S just west of Champion. Follow 980S to McDonald. Turn right on SR4012 to Primrose. Trailhead parking and access is at the intersection of John's Rd. and Noblestown Rd.

For access in Carnegie, take I-79 south to Noblestown Road and head 1.7 miles west to Walker's Mill. Turn left on Walker's Mill Road at the red barn, then 0.1 mile to parking lot on the right.

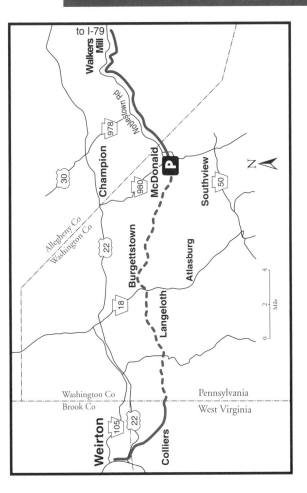

Location: Allegheny and Washington Counties, PA and
Brook County, WV
Miles: 29 miles, 11 improved
Endpoints: McDonald, PA to Weirton, WV
Surface: Crushed limestone
Contact: Andy Baechle
Washington County Department of Parks and
Recreation
100 West Beau St - Room 604
Washington, PA 15301
724-228-6867

Penns Creek Path

Penns Creek Path follows part of the Mid-State Trail, a cross-country hiking trail that traverses four state forests and eight natural areas in the ridge and valley region of central Pennsylvania.

The main trail parallels the route of the old Penns Creek Indian Path and follows along the border of Huntingdon and Centre counties for more than 166 miles. The rail-trail section follows the abandoned railroad located in Poe Paddy State Park. Built in 1879, it linked all the small timber railroads that ran through the mountain valleys. Poe Paddy is located on the site of Poe Mills, a prosperous, short-lived lumber town of the 1880s and 1890s. There was also an excursion train that looped from Milroy to Poe Paddy in the 1900s. The railroad was abandoned in 1970.

Poe Valley State Park is located 1.5 miles east of Potters Mills on US 322, near the top of Seven Mountains Scenic Area. Follow marked State Forest roads for 10 miles to Poe Valley. The roads leading to the park are not entirely paved.

Nearby, Bald Eagle State Forest offers four additional rail-trails. The Brush Hollow, Buffalo Flat, Chestnut Flat, and Duncan Trails traverse rugged terrain on turn-of-the-century rail corridors. R.B. Winter State Park, in Bald Eagle State Forest, is located on PA 192, west of Mifflinburg. Visit the park office for further information.

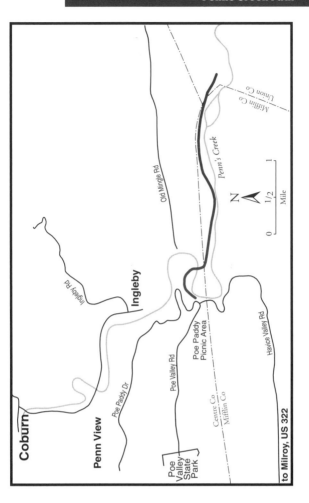

 on certain sections

Location: Centre, Mifflin and Snyder Counties
Miles: 3.6
Endpoints: Poe Paddy State Park to Cherry Run
Surface: Original ballast
Contact: Thomas T. Thwaites
Mid State Trail Association
PO Box 167
Boalsburg, PA 16827
814-237-7703

Perkiomen Trail

The Perkiomen Trail (PT) is a 19.5-mile multi-use Trail extending from its connection to the Schuylkill River Trail (SRT) in Oaks in Upper Providence Township to Green Lane Park in Upper Frederick Township. Most of the Trail is surfaced with cinder and packed gravel. The Trail serves as a regional access between Green Lane Park in Green Lane, Central Perkiomen Valley Park in Schwenksville and Lower Perkiomen Valley Park in Oaks and two very significant sites, the Mill Grove Landmark in Audubon and Pennypacker Mills Site in Schwenksville.

The Perkiomen Trail is in various stages of acquisition, planning, design and construction. Please note that the entire trail is not fully developed and available for use. Sections of the proposed trail have not yet been improved to safely accommodate trail users. Also note that unopened sections may exist because the County may have not yet acquired trail easements from landowners, and people passing through these lands might be trespassing on private property.

To access the Perkiomen Trail at the Camp Rainbow site, take the PA Turnpike to exit 326 — Valley Forge. Follow 202 South less than one mile to 422 West. Follow 422 West past the Oaks and exit on 29 North. Follow 29 North through Collegeville and on to Schwenksville. Proceed north on 29 and go right at the hardware store on Spring Mountain Road. Proceed to Spring Mt. Village and go right at the three-way intersection and the Spring Mountain Hotel. Cross the bridge and go left at the ski hill on Clemmers Hill Road. Proceed up the hill and go left onto Haim Road. Continue on to Camp Rainbow.

To access the trail in Perkiomenville, follow 29 North past Schwenksville and bear right in Zieglerville to follow 29 North on to Perkiomenville. Go right on Crusher Road at the big mill. Then go right immediately and continue .25 miles to the trailhead.

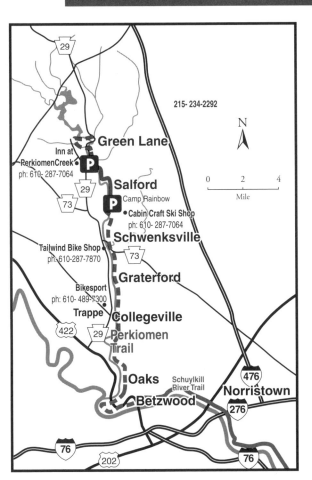

Location: Montgomery County
Miles: 19.5, 4.5 open
Endpoints: Oaks to Green Lane
Surface: crushed cinder
Contact: John H. Wood
Montgomery County Planning Commission
Montgomery County Courthouse
PO Box 311
Norristown, PA 19404-0311
610-278-3736
www.montcopa.org/plan.com

Pine Creek Trail

The Jersey Shore, Pine Creek & Buffalo Railroad began in 1883 by carrying timber to sawmills in Tiadaghton, Cammal, and Slate Run, located along the floor of Pine Creek Gorge. The railroad also transported coal north to New York State and by 1896 was carrying seven million tons of freight and three passenger trains on daily runs between Wellsboro Junction and Williamsport.

The last freight train passed through the gorge on in October 1988, thus ending more than a century of service.

One of the most spectacular natural areas in the Commonwealth, the Pine Creek Gorge is often referred to as the Grand Canyon of Pennsylvania. It was recognized as a National Natural Landmark in 1969.

With 41 miles of developed trail, the corridor hugs Pine Creek for 62 miles, providing access to whitewater rafting and canoeing in the spring, and great views of dramatic rock outcrops and numerous waterfalls. You may be lucky enough to see an eagle, osprey, or coyote, or catch a glimpse of a deer, wild turkey, heron, hawk, or one of the river otters recently reintroduced to the area.

Horseback riding is allowed. To use the path beside the new trail surface between Ansonia and Tiadaghton, equestrians should park at the Ansonia Trailhead.

Near Ansonia, park at Darlington Run on Route 362 just before its intersection with Route 6; or turn left at the intersection of Routes 6 and 362, cross the bridge over Pine Creek (and trail) and take an immediate right onto SR3022. The parking lot is on the right.

Or, park at Rattlesnake Rock on Route 414, two miles south of Blackwell. A small parking lot is avalable at Blackwell.

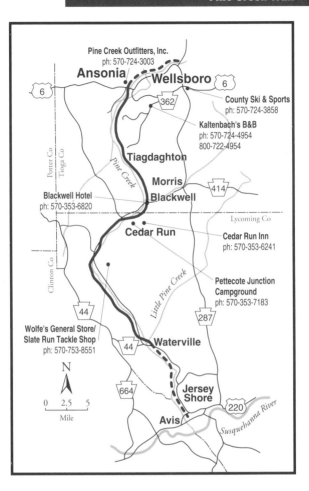

Pine Creek Outfitters, Inc.
ph: 570-724-3003

Ansonia

Wellsboro

6 | 6

County Ski & Sports
ph: 570-724-3858

362

Kaltenbach's B&B
ph: 570-724-4954
800-722-4954

Tiagdaghton

Morris

414

Blackwell Hotel
ph: 570-353-6820

Blackwell

Lycoming Co

Cedar Run

Cedar Run Inn
ph: 570-353-6241

Pettecote Junction
Campground
ph: 570-353-7183

44

287

Wolfe's General Store/
Slate Run Tackle Shop
ph: 570-753-8551

44

Waterville

N

664

**Jersey
Shore**

220

Avis

Susquehanna River

0   2.5   5
Mile

Potter Co / Tioga Co

Pine Creek

Clinton Co

Little Pine Creek

Location:	Tioga and Lycoming Counties
Miles:	41
Endpoints:	Ansonia to Waterville
Surface:	Crushed limestone
Contact:	Bureau of Forestry
	Tioga State Forest
	Wellsboro, PA 16901
	570-724-2868

Plainfield Township Trail

Once used to transport slate from nearby quarries, the Bangor and Portland Railway opened in 1880 and served the Delaware, Lackawanna and Western's main line at Portland.

A formal merger of the Bangor and Portland and the Delaware, Lackawanna and Western Railroad occurred on July 1, 1909. One of the last branches to operate steam locomotives, the Bangor Engine Terminal withdrew its last steam locomotive on January 5, 1953.

The railroad was bought by Conrail in 1976, and then abandoned in 1981. It was sold to Plainfield Township in 1987 and converted to a trail.

A breathtaking view of a 70-foot drop into the Bushkill Creek is just one of the features this trail has to offer. Traversing the entire length of the township, the 60-foot wide right-of-way may eventually link at least seven other trails, including the Appalachian Trail, to create a corridor from the Lehigh and Delaware Valleys to the Poconos.

For now, there are miles of rural landscapes and beautiful views to behold as you wind your way through the countryside and over the Bushkill's five bridges.

To reach the Belfast Junction parking lot, take the Stockertown Exit off of Route 33 and make a right at the first stop sign. At the next traffic light, turn left onto Sullivan Trail Road. Travel .75 mile. The trailhead parking lot will be on your right, just after a power station.

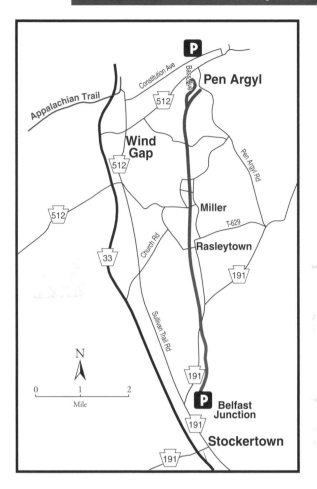

Location: Northampton County
Miles: 6.7
Endpoints: Plainfield Township to Pen Argyl
Surface: Crushed stone
Contact: Ginny Koehler
Plainfield Township
6292 Sullivan Trail
Nazareth, PA 18064
610-759-6944

Pymatuning State Park Trail

The word "Pymatuning" is derived from the Iroquois language, probably from the Seneca tribe, meaning "the crooked-mouthed man's dwelling place." This saying may refer to the Erie tribe, which previously lived in the area and was ruled by a queen known for her cunning.

The trail is located on the abandoned Erie and Pittsburgh branch of the Pennsylvania Railroad and is partially located in Pymatuning State Park. The park was created in 1931 as plans to dam Pymatuning Lake were finalized. Today, it is a very popular two-state recreational area.

Although the trail is short, 2.3 miles in length, points of interest located adjacent to it make it a worthwhile experience. The trail is notable for passing the Pymatuning Lake spillway where you can feed the fish and geese that cluster there. You'll also find a waterfowl museum and fish hatchery with visitor centers at both locations. At the visitor centers, you can learn about the many species that are protected in the 2,500-acre wildlife refuge adjacent to the lake. These facilities are generally open from late spring through early fall.

The trailhead is located one mile south of Linesville — off Linesville/Hartstown Road located between Route 6 and SR 285.

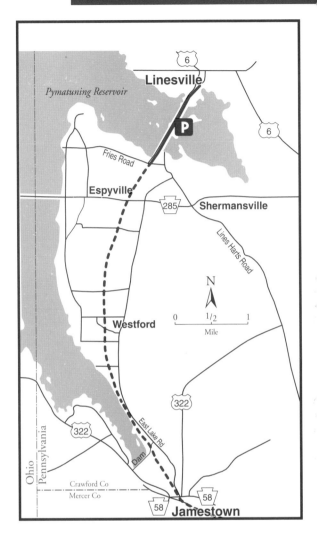

Location: Crawford County
Miles: 2.3
Endpoints: Pymatuning State Park
Surface: Cinder, grass
Contact: Pymatuning State Park
PO Box 425
Jamestown, PA 16134
724-932-3141
www.dcnr.state.pa.us

Roaring Run Trail

The Roaring Run Trail was built on the abandoned Pennsylvania Railroad Apollo Industrial Track which was built on the abandoned Pennsylvania West Branch Canal. Today, portions of the canal can still be seen from the trail.

The Roaring Run Watershed Association was formed in 1982 to help preserve this historic area and clean up pollution from abandoned mines. The right-of-way was donated to the association and opened as a trail in 1989.

Beginning at the parking area on Canal Road, the Roaring Run Trail parallels the Kiskiminetas River to the southeast. At the 1.5-mile mark, the remains of canal Lock No. 15 can be seen. Directly out from these remains once stood a 16-foot high dam which was destroyed by a flood in 1866. During low water some remains are visible.

Take the PA Turnpike to Exit 75 — the New Stanton exit. Follow the PA Turnpike Route 66 extension to its end in Delmont. Follow Route 66 North to Apollo. Make a right at the light after crossing the bridge and follow Kiski Ave .7 miles to Cherry Lane. Continue on Cherry Lane to a fork and bend right on Canal Road. Proceed to parking at the end of the road.

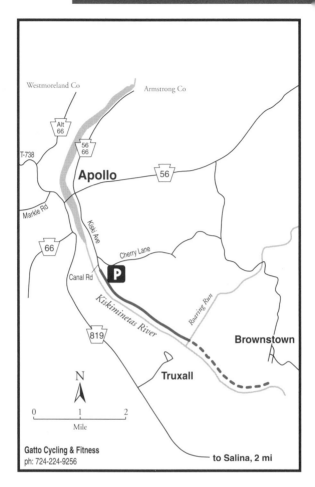

Gatto Cycling & Fitness
ph: 724-224-9256

to Salina, 2 mi

Location: Armstrong County
Miles: 3.7, 2.0 improved
Endpoints: Canal Road to Roaring Run
Surface: Crushed limestone
Contact: Andy Schreffler
Roaring Run Watershed Association
215 Rovel Street
Apollo, PA 15686
724-568-1483

Samuel Justus Recreational Trail

Connecting Oil City and Franklin, the Samuel Justus Recreational Trail is a six mile segment of a 30-mile trail that follows what was originally the Allegheny Valley Railroad.

The "A.V." was completed to Oil City in 1868 and connected the oil fields with Pittsburgh. It operated as an independent company until it was absorbed into the Pennsylvania Railroad system in 1910. The line was abandoned by Conrail in 1984.

The trail begins across the Allegheny River from Franklin, which is known for its well-preserved Victorian architecture and tree-lined streets. The trail follows the river north toward Oil City through lush woodlands, passing iron furnaces, several operating oil wells, Pioneer Cemetery, an orchard planted by Johnny Appleseed, and a visitors center located in an 1844 Salt Box house.

The trail's paved surface is perfect for bicycling and in-line skating. You may also want to visit the mansion of Senator Joseph Sibley, who made his fortune by inventing the first formula for refining crude oil.

To access the trail in Franklin, follow I-80 to Exit 29. Follow Rt 8 North to Rt 322. Follow 322 East / 8th Street through Franklin. After crossing the Allegheny River on the 8th Street Bridge, park at the trailhead located on the right.

To access the trail in Oil City, follow I-80 to Exit 29. Follow Rt 8 North, crossing the intersection with Rt 322, and continue to follow Rt 8 / Rt 62 to Oil City. Cross the Allegheny River on the Petroleum Street Bridge. Continue to the second light, and head right on West 1st Street. Continue about 1.5 miles to trailhead parking on the right, just past the GPU building.

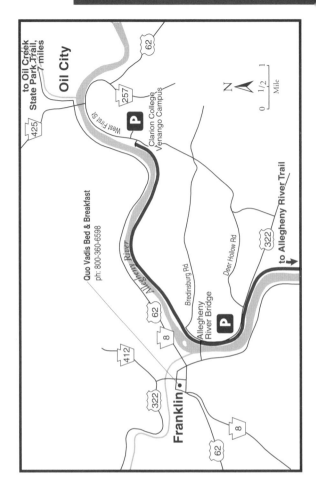

Location: Venango County
Miles: 6.0
Endpoints: Franklin to Oil City
Surface: Asphalt
Contact: Cranberry Township
                  PO Box 378
                  Seneca, PA 16346
                  814-676-8812

Schuylkill River Trail

The Schuylkill River Trail stretches 25 miles along the historic Schuylkill River from downtown Philadelphia at the Philadelphia Museum of Art to Valley Forge National Historical Park. The multi-use trail, a joint effort between the City of Philadelphia and Montgomery County, is designed for bicyclists, walkers, joggers and rollerbladers. In Philadelphia, the trail uses Fairmount Park trails and the Manyunk Canal towpath. In Montgomery County, the trail utilizes an abandoned Pennsylvania Railroad line. At its terminus at Valley Forge you can continue traveling north by linking at Betzwood with Valley Forge Historical Park trails. Future developments will soon extend the trail into the Phoenixville area of Chester County. Eventually, the trail will connect to Berks and Schuykill Counties to create more than 100 continuous miles of rail-trails along the Schuylkill River from Philadelphia to the coal regions near Pottsville.

The nearby Perkiomen Creek Trail (see page 122) will soon stretch from the Schuylkill River Trail along the Reading Line 25.5 miles to Upper Hanover Township and possibly link with Berks County.

The river was once a major transportation resource that played a key role in the region's development. The trail is the spine of the Schuylkill River Heritage Corridor - a five county area designated as a state Heritage Park - which highlights the rich industrial and cultural heritage of the region. The trail traverses beautiful scenic ridges and stream valleys, historic villages, and boroughs while it offers easy access to various business, cultural and shopping center districts.

To reach Valley Forge National Historical Park, take the Pennsylvania Turnpike to Exit 326 (Valley Forge) — or old Exit 24. Take US 422 west to Audubon/Trooper exit and turn left off the exit ramp. You'll find parking for the Schuylkill River Trail at Betzwood just ahead on the right.

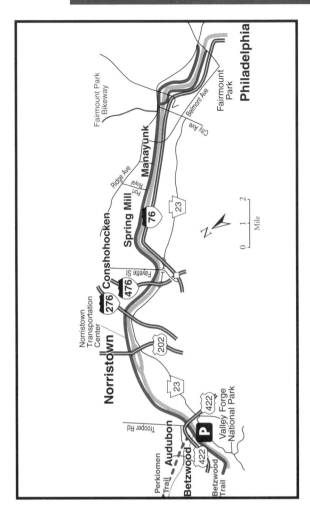

Location: Philadelphia and Montgomery Counties
Miles: 25
Endpoints: Philadelphia to Valley Forge
Surface: Asphalt
Contact: John H. Wood
Montgomery County Planning Commission
Montgomery County Courthouse
PO Box 311
Norristown, PA 19404-0311
610-278-3736
www.montcopa.org/plan.com

Sentiero di Shay

Located in the northwest corner of Lycoming County near the village of Slate Run, the Black Forest was named for the dense, dark coniferous forests that originally covered the region. Now a part of the Tiadaghton State Forest, the Black Forest Trail system is a 42-mile series of loop trails comprised partially of the remains of the Cammal and Black Forest Railroad, the Slate Run Railroad and logging roads.

The Sentiero di Shay trail (whose name translates from Italian as "path of Shay") pays tribute to the Italian laborers who hand-built the railroad grade so that timber might be transported by rugged Shay engines.

Primarily a cross-country ski route, this 13.4 mile trail can also be enjoyed for hiking. You'll pass oak, white birch, pitch pine, several aspen meadows, streams and hollows, a spruce corridor, and other diverse hardwoods. Along the way, the Sentiero di Shay shares the railroad corridor with other cross-country ski trails, the George B. Will Trail and the Ruth Will Trail. Mr. Will was a ranger for the Forest Service who is credited with introducing cross-country skiing to the area in 1914 on skis imported from Sweden. Much of the Black Forest had been cut over by that time and George recalled that "you could see for miles."

Joining the Black Forest Trail System and the Susquehannock Trail System, are the North and South Link Trails, 9.3 and 6 miles respectively. Built almost exclusively on abandoned railroad grades, the Link Trails help provide a roughly 26-mile (two or three day) backpacking loop traversing three counties, numerous water courses, and countless cross trails and abandoned railroad grades.

To reach the trailhead, take PA44 slightly more than one-half mile south of Slate Run Road, 34 miles south of Coudersport. The trail begins at the trailhead for the Black-berry Trail, designated by a carved wooden sign. The Sentiero di Shay is blazed with blue circles.

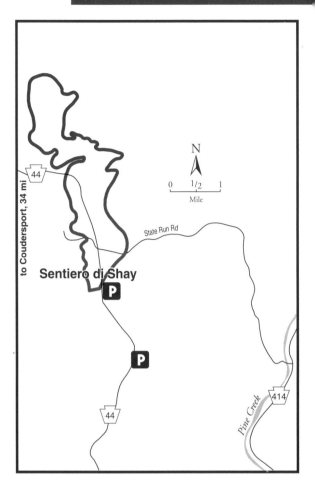

Location: Lycoming County
Miles: 13.4
Endpoints: Within Tiadaghton State Forest
Surface: Grass
Contact: Tiadaghton State Forest
Bureau of Forestry
423 East Central Avenue
South Williamsport, PA 17701
570-327-3450

Shenango Trail

The Shenango Trail once served as a towpath along the Erie Canal Extension. During the mid-1800s, mules pulled boats along the canal, linking goods from the Great Lakes to Pittsburgh and beyond. Recognizing the geographic significance of such a link, Andrew Carnegie formed a conglomerate group to lease the nearby lines for 999 years. Even today, as much of the railroad industry has fallen, tremendous quantities of freight still travel along the tracks.

In addition to the structural and historical details of the canal and towpath, the Shenango Trail offers a wealth of natural attractions. Many species of both plants and animals thrive in the region. The nearby Seth Meyers Trail is only .5 miles long, but it offers the opportunity to take a self-guided hike and learn more about nature. More recreational activities are available at the Shenango River Lake Area.

Near the trail's northern terminus stands the Kidd's Mill Covered Bridge, the only covered bridge in Mercer County, and the only Smith truss covered bridge in Pennsylvania.

To access the Shenango Trail at Kidd's Mill Bridge, Follow Route 18 north from Sharon. Cross the bridge and continue 3.5 miles to Crestview Road. Turn right on Crestview and continue for .5 miles. The trailhead is at the bridge.

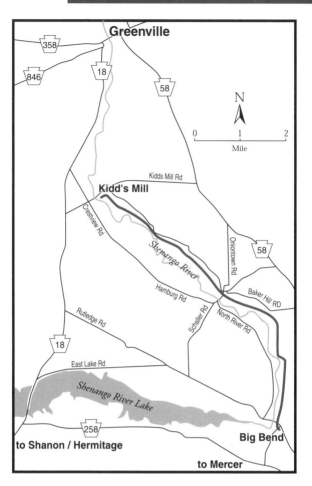

Location: Mercer County
Miles: 7.5
Endpoints: Kidd's Mill Covered Bridge to Big Bend
Surface: Cinder
Contact: US Army Corps of Engineers
Shenango River Lake District
724-962-7746

Stavich Bicycle Trail

This 12-mile trail was constructed in 1983 with the help of donations from the Stavich family and local individuals.

The Stavich Trail is unusual for two reasons. First, unlike most rail-trails, it was built on an abandoned interurban electric railroad right-of-way: the Penn-Ohio line which was abandoned in 1933. Interurbans were not built to the stringent standards of conventional railroads, so you'll encounter more grades than you might on an ordinary rail-trail.

The Stavich's second notable feature is the fact that it is one of the few rail-trails in the country that connects two states. This gently rolling trail will take you from Struthers, Ohio to near New Castle, Pennsylvania.

Running along the Mahoning River, this mostly rural trail also parallels the CSX railroad main line. The asphalt-paved trail is great for bicycling, in-line skating, walking and is accessible for persons with disabilities.

The Stavich Trail is a rail-*with*-trail — the trail shares right-of-way with an active rail line. Rail-with-trails have become quite popular with nine other such facilities in Pennsylvania and a total of 61 rail-with-trails across the nation. Recent detailed research from RTC suggests rail-with-trails to offer communities both safe and enjoyable recreation and transportation.

On the Pennsylvania side, exit off Route 60 at State Street. (Route 224 east) Take a right on Scotland Lane and a right on Washington Drive. Washington Drive leads to the trailhead.

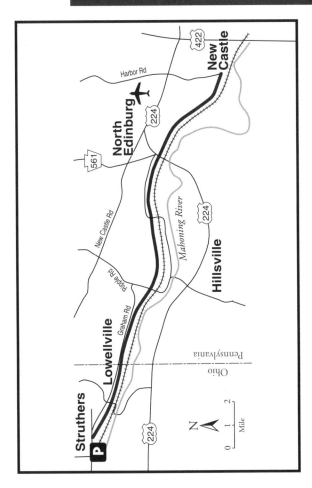

Location: Lawrence (PA) and Mahoning (OH) Counties

Miles: 12

Endpoints: New Castle, PA to Struthers, OH

Surface: Asphalt

Contact: JoAnne McBride
Lawrence County Tourism Bureau
229 South Jefferson Street
New Castle, PA 16101
724-654-8408

Stony Valley Railroad Grade

Named St. Anthony's Wilderness by Moravian missionaries who came in 1742 to convert native tribes, the Stony Creek valley became the site of five bustling towns after discovery of coal in 1824. The 1850s saw the construction of the Schuylkill & Susquehanna Railroad, built to transport coal to the canals and tourists to Cold Springs' famous mineral water. So popular was the spring water that a 200-room resort was built to accommodate the wealthy Philadelphians who came for the healing waters.

By 1944, the mines were exhausted, the lumber stripped, the railroad abandoned, and the hotel burned as the last residents left. The Pennsylvania Game Commission purchased the land in 1945 and converted the railroad to a trail soon after, making the Stony Valley Railroad Grade one of the nation's first rail-trails.

Located in 44,342 acres of state game land, the forest has rebounded in a remarkable way, providing habitat for an abundance of animals and preserving what remains of the mining towns. The foundation and stone steps to the old Cold Springs Hotel stand shaded by towering Norway spruces originally planted by hotel landscapers. For those seeking foilage without sweat, each fall the Stony Valley Railroad Grade is open to motor vehicles for one day.

Take 22/322 north from Harrisburg, exiting at Route 225 into Dauphin. Just after the exit, the road veers left and crosses Stony Creek. Turn right onto Stony Creek Road and follow it for 5 miles to what appears to be a cul-de-sac. At the top of the cul-de-sac's loop is a dirt road off to the right. Stay on this dirt road to the trailhead. With a massive PennDOT construction project still under way in the area, connecting roadways may move or cease to exist.

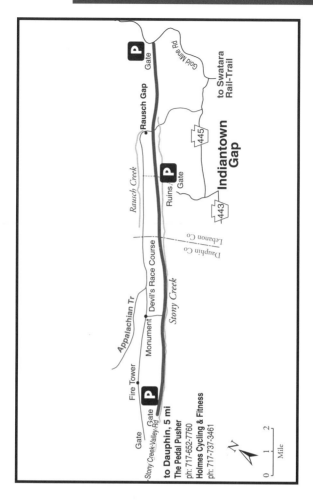

Location: Dauphin, Lebanon and Schuylkill Counties
Miles: 18
Endpoints: Dauphin to Gold Mine Rd.
Surface: Packed cinder/dirt
Contact: Roland Bergner, Chief
Federal/State Coordination Division
Pennsylvania Game Commission
2001 Elmerton Avenue
Harrisburg, PA 17110-9797
717-787-9612

Struble Trail

Originally a branch of the Pennsylvania Railroad, a portion of the abandoned right-of-way was converted into a trail by the Chester County Parks & Recreation Department and dedicated in 1979. Today the 2.5-mile trail attracts over 67,000 visitors each year. The county hopes to extend the trail to include 13.5 more miles.

Paralleling the east branch of Brandywine Creek, the Struble Trail provides a perfect setting for amateur naturalists and wonderful opportunities for joggers, and bicyclists. Equestrians are welcome on the undeveloped sections of the trail.

While you're in the area, you may want to visit the other parks located in Chester County. Hibernia County Park offers 800 acres of woodlands and meadows for picnicking and camping. There are plenty of good fishing spots along the west branch of Brandywine Creek and the children's pond stocked with trout from the park's nursery. There are also seasonal tours of Hibernia Mansion, an ironmaster's county home listed on the National Register of Historic Places.

Springton Manor Farm, which was part of William Penn Manor, is also included in the National Register of Historic Places and is a tourist demonstration farm that includes animal petting areas and an agricultural museum.

From US Route 30 Bypass traveling west, exit at Route 282 near Downingtown. Turn left off the exit, proceed under the Route 30 bridge. The trailhead is the second drive on the right. From US Route 30 Bypass traveling east, exit at US322, turn right and go to Pennsylvania Avenue in Downingtown. Turn left and proceed to another left on PA282. Turn right onto Norwood Road; the trailhead is the first left.

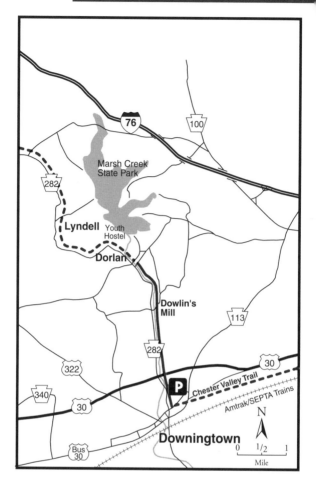

 on certain sections

Location: Chester County

Miles: 2.5

Endpoints: Downingtown to Dorlan

Surface: Asphalt

Contact: Chester County Parks & Recreation
601 Westtown Road, Suite 160
P.O. Box 2747
West Chester, PA 19380-0990
610-344-6415
www.chesco.org/ccparks

Susquehannock Trail System

Located in scenic Potter and Clinton Counties, the Susquehannock Hiking Trail is an 85 mile amalgamation of old Civilian Conservation Corps fire trails, logging roads and railroad grades through the Susquehannock State Forest. Isolated and pristine, the Susquehannock Trail System provides hikers and backpackers with a well marked (orange blaze) rugged trail with some steep grades on single track tread in an isolated backcountry setting. The Hammersley Wild Area is especially unspoiled, offering the longest section of roadless trail in the Susquehannock loop. Please take note: the STS accepts foot-traffic only.

Somewhat coincidentally, the Hammersley is also the most rail-intensive portion of the system. Timber was cut here between 1906 and 1910. Several logging camps and a small town were once located near where Nelson Branch and Hammersley Fork merge. Also, this site is just north of the Forrest H. Dutlinger Natural Area, a 1,500 acre preserve which includes a 158-acre stand of old growth timber (primarily hemlocks).

To access the trails, take Route 6 to the Susquehannock State Forest District Office, about two miles.

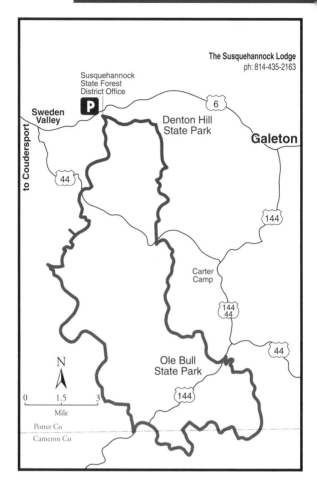

Location: Potter and Clinton Counties
Miles: Roughly 30 miles of rail-trail
Endpoints: Loop trail in Susquehannock State Forest
Surface: Grass and dirt
Contact: David Schiller
Susquehannock State Forest
Bureau of Forestry
3150 East 2nd St.
PO Box 673
Coudersport, PA 16915-0673
814-274-3600

Swatara Rail-Trail

After European settlement in the 1750s, anthracite coal was discovered in the Tremont area. As the demand for coal exploded through the 1820s, the Union Canal was constructed to connect the Schuylkill and Susquehanna and improve anthracite supply transport. From Lebanon, a branch canal was constructed to Pine Grove through what is now Swatara State Park.

The Flood of 1862 destroyed the canal. Since the operation of the Lebanon – Tremont Branch of the Reading Railroad on the opposite bank of Swatara Creek served all transport needs, the canal was never repaired.

The Swatara Rail-Trail stretches the length of Swatara Creek from Pine Grove almost to Lickdale — revealing remnants of both the canal and the railroad. Even though the path is somewhat close to I-81, the combination of lush forest and rugged trail tread creates a sense of remoteness perfect for the adventure-lover. Nearby the Stony Valley Railroad Grade offers another backcountry treat; an extended day or weekend excursion may be in order. Also, a connection with the Appalachian Trail can be found near Inwood.

To access the Swatara Creek Trail near Lickdale, travel north on I-81 from Harrisburg about 20 miles to Exit 90. Head towards Lebanon. At the first light, continue straight, past the gas station and take a left into the campground parking lot. Primitive parking and trailhead access can be found past the camp store at the gate.

Currently the trail is in a rough state and trailhead access on the east side of the Swatara Rail-Trail is difficult to locate.

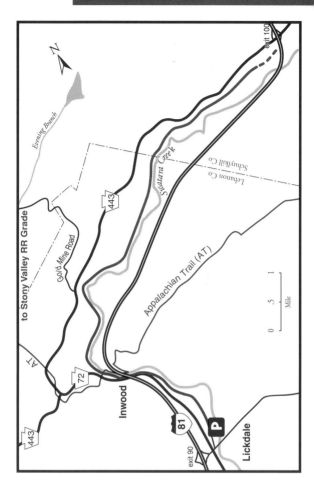

Location: Lebanon and Schuylkill Counties
Miles: 15 miles
Endpoints: I-81 Exit 90, Exit 100
Surface: Unimproved (often wet)
Contact: Swatara State Park
R.R. 1 Box 7045
Grantville, PA 17028-9682
717-865-6470
www.dcnr.state.pa.us

Switchback Railroad Trail

The Switchback Railroad was the second railroad operating in America and the first in Pennsylvania when it opened. Built to haul coal from the Summit Mine to the Lehigh Canal, the railroad evolved from a gravity and mule-powered system to a 95% gravity-run operation (with the help of two steam engines).

Although the cars ceased carrying coal in 1932, they continued to haul people, who came to enjoy the thrilling ride. Thomas Edison was one of those people, as was the builder of the first rollercoaster. A popular tourist attraction for 59 years, the Switchback was sold for scrap in 1937 and converted to a trail in 1977.

Traversing the valley with Pisgah Mountain to the north and Mauch Chunk Ridge to the south, the trail loops down into Jim Thorpe and back up the valley to Summit Hill. Oak, hickory, and birch are found in the lower section of the valley; white pine and hemlock are nestled between the high mountain ridges. In these areas, you may observe black bear, wild turkey, porcupine, weasel, and maybe even a wildcat. Fields and streams along the trail support deer, ruffed grouse, woodchuck, red and gray foxes, beaver, and pheasant.

To access the Switchback, take US209 to Jim Thorpe. Park at the railroad station downtown. Travel a few blocks west on Broadway, then turn right at the Opera House on the appropriately named Hill Road. In less than half a mile uphill, you will turn left onto the trail. Or follow Broadway uphill less than a mile and pick up the Switchback Trail on the left where Broadway crosses Mauch Chunk Creek.

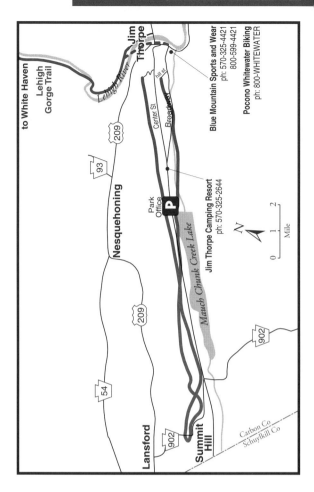

Location: Carbon County
Miles: 15
Endpoints: Summit Hill to Jim Thorpe
Surface: Original ballast
Contact: Mauch Chunk Lake Park Office
          Carbon County Parks & Recreation
          625 Lentz Trail Road
          Jim Thorpe, PA 18229-1902
          570-325-3669
          www.dcnr.state.pa.us

Three Rivers Heritage Trail System

The Three Rivers Heritage Trail System begins on Washington's Landing, a 42-acre island in the Allegheny River. Once known as Herr's Island and a stopover for livestock trains between Chicago and the East Coast, Herr's Island has been undergoing renovation since the 1980s. Its slaughterhouses and scrap yards have been replaced by office buildings, a marina, tennis courts, and a trail circling the island. Traveling down the Allegheny to the Ohio River, past North Shore Park and the Carnegie Science Center, then crossing the Ohio and proceeding up the Monongahela River past Station Square and Southside Riverfront Park, it's easy to see how the Three Rivers Heritage Trail System will link the most dynamic geographic and historical features of this vibrant city. Offering precisely the kind of transportation alternatives to which Rails-to-Trails Conservancy and its supporting organizations are most committed, the Three Rivers Heritage Trail System will also provide a vital link to the Pittsburgh to Washington, DC trail sought for completion by mid 2004.

There are presently three sections of trail completed, totaling 7 miles. The largest section of 3.5 miles runs from just beyond the Carnegie Science Center to Washington's Landing.

To access the trail from points south of Pittsburgh, take Interstate 279 North to Exit 5B. At the traffic signal after coming off the ramp, continue straight on Reedsdale Ave. Do NOT take the Sproat Way left turn. Continue to the next left, and follow this turnaround onto North Shore Ave. Stay in the right lane. Turn right on Allegheny Ave., and turn right again into the Carnegie Science Center parking lot.

At Washington's Landing a pedestrian/bicycling bridge leads to the island, which another mile of trail encircles. Parking is available on Washington's Landing.

For the 2.5-mile Southside segment, take East Carson Street to 18th Street and turn toward the river. Cross the tracks and turn right to parking just after the boat ramp.

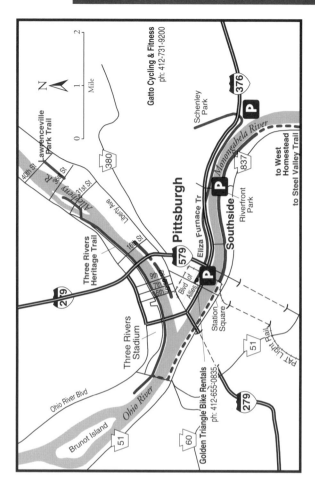

Location: Allegheny County

Miles: 7 miles

Endpoints: Washington's Landing to beyond the Carnegie Science Center

Surface: Crushed limestone and asphalt

Contact: John Stephen
Friends of the Riverfront
PO Box 42434
Pittsburgh, PA 15203
412-488-0212
www.atatrail.org

Thun Trail

A segment of the regional Schuylkill River Trail, the Thun (pronounced "Tune") Trail follows the former Pennsylvania Railroad Schuylkill Branch built along the route of the historic Schuylkill Canal. Near the trail in Gibraltar is the Allegheny Aqueduct, a stone structure built in 1824 to carry the Schuylkill Canal across the Allegheny Creek. Beautiful railroad bridges, built in 1918, provide impressive views of the Schuylkill River and surrounding hills. Paralleling Routes 422 and 724, the Thun Trail offers an alternate route for commuters and beautiful views for those seeking leisure activities. Currently 4 miles of trail are open with work on the remaining sections under design.

To reach the Brentwood Drive trailhead, take Route 10 (Morgantown Road) .9 mile east from the intersection of Routes 222 (Lancaster Avenue) and 10.

The Angstadt Lane trailhead is just east of the intersection of Route 724 and Interstate 176.

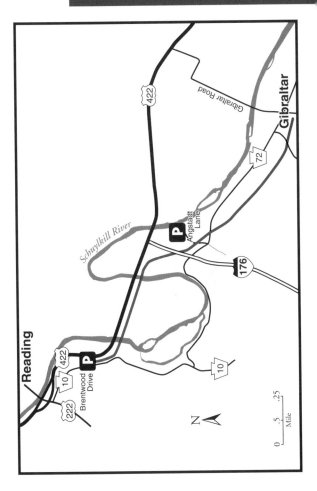

Location: Berks County
Miles: 10.0, 4 improved
Endpoints: Reading to Gibraltar
Surface: Crushed stone
Contact: Dixie Swenson
Schuylkill River Greenway Association
960 Old Mill Road
Wyomissing, PA 19610
610-372-3916
info@schuylkillriver.org
www.schuylkillriver.org

Towpath Bike Trail

Three modes of transportation once operated on the Towpath Bike Trail: the Lehigh Canal, the Central Railroad of New Jersey (Easton and Western branch), and the Lehigh Valley Transit interurban.

Chartered in 1818, the privately-owned canal remained in operation for 113 years. It hauled anthracite coal from Mauch Chunk to the Delaware Canal at Easton. The Easton and Western branch was built in 1914 and abandoned in 1972. The LVT Easton line was part of a larger electric railway system that stretched from the Delaware Water Gap to near Philadelphia.

The trail — formerly known as the "National Trails Towpath Bike Trail of Palmer and Bethlehem Townships" — served as one of 10 model rail-trail facilities during the Carter Administration. The trail hosts 70,000 people annually, the majority coming from Palmer and Bethlehem Townships, as well as residents of Northampton and Lehigh Counties. Nearly 30 percent of the trail users are people commuting to and from work, school, shopping areas, and parks.

This eight-foot wide asphalt trail starts near the Easton Area High School and traverses a variety of landscapes, including forests, farmland, residential neighborhoods, and the banks of the Lehigh River. The trail also provided some land along the river, which is now Riverview Park, a popular fishing area that provides access to the Delaware and Lehigh Canal National Heritage Corridor.

Plan to see improvements on the Lehigh Canal and the abandoned rail line between the Towpath Bike Trail and the Lehigh Canal soon. Currently, though, both paths are being used as part of the Route 33 construction project.

For parking at Riverview Park, take US Route 22 East from SR33 to 25th Street South. Stay on 25th Street South for about two miles and turn right on Lehigh Street. Turn right into the parking lot. Continue across the one-way Glendon Bridge into Hugh Moore Park for additional parking as well as access to the Delaware Canal Towpath.

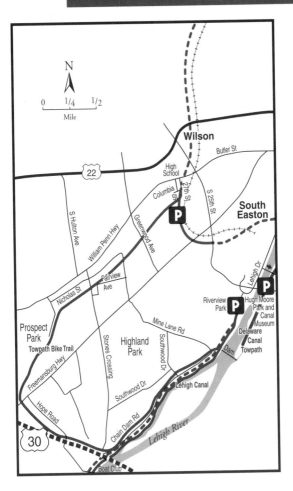

Location: Northampton County
Miles: 11.3
Endpoints: Bethlehem to Palmer
Surface: Asphalt
Contact: Ted Sales
Palmer Township Board of Supervisors
PO Box 3039
Palmer, PA 18043-3039
610-253-7191

Warren-North Warren Bike Trail

Located along the banks of the Conewango Creek, the open two mile segment of this proposed four mile trail follows an old New York Central branch north from the City of Warren. Designed to serve first as a safe alternative for cyclists and commuters from the downtown area to a burgeoning business district along Route 62, the Warren-North Warren Bike Trail will also serve to preserve the scenic vistas of the Conewango and control flooding along its tributary, Jackson Run.

The railroad corridor followed by the Warren-North Warren Trail was built to provide rail service to the several oil refineries which once occupied this area. The existing trail follows the banks of the beautiful Conewango Creek.

Follow Business Route 6 (Pennsylvania Ave) until intersecting with Market Street. Follow Market Street to 5th Ave. Turn right on 5th Ave. Turn left on East St. and continue to the end of the road. To reach the other trailhead, continue north on Route 62 to Jackson Street in North Warren.

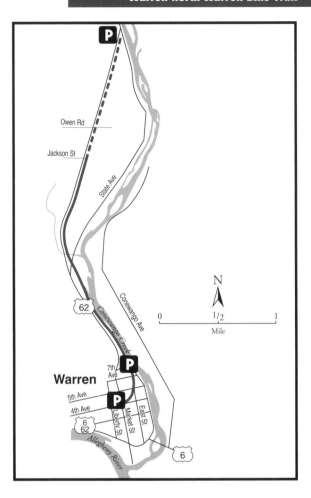

Location: Warren County

Miles: 2

Endpoints: Warren to North Warren

Surface: Asphalt

Contact: Dan Glotz
Warren County Planning &
Zoning Commission
207 W. 5th Ave
Warren, PA 16365
814-726-3861

Youghiogheny River Trail (North)

Built in 1883, the Pittsburgh, McKeesport and Youghiogheny hauled coal and coke from the rich Connellsville District to the steel mills of Pittsburgh. Nicknamed the "P-Mickey" for its initials, P. McK. & Y., it was merged into the Pittsburgh and Lake Erie Railroad in 1965 and became known as the Connellsville Branch.

The freight and coal traffic that sustained the branch dried up by the mid-1980s and the line was abandoned in 1990. It was immediately purchased by the Regional Trail Corporation, a three-county consortium that is operating the trail.

The development of this north section of the Youghiogheny River Trail (YRT) will help complete a multi-state rail-trail system linking Pittsburgh to Washington, DC. The trail is especially suited to long-distance leisure trips, since the rise in elevation is no more than 100 feet for the entire trail.

To access the trail in Smithton, take I-70 to the Smithton Exit and follow signage to Smithton. Then turn right on Rt981. Turn right at the first sign on Main Street — still following Rt981. Cross the Yough and turn right immediately to trailhead access at milepoint 39.2.

To access the trail at milepoint 58 in Connellsville, follow Rt119 South from Pittsburgh to Rt711. Head left on Rt711 to Third Street. Head left on Third and continue to 50-car trailhead parking lot near Riverfront Park. In the town of Connellsville, the YRT follows Third Street. Head north on Third to access the YRT North towards Pittsburgh or access the YRT South towards Cumberland, Md.

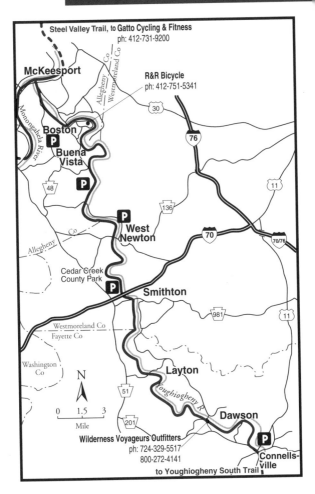

Location: Allegheny, Fayette and
Westmoreland Counties

Miles: 43 miles

Endpoints: Connellsville to McKeesport

Surface: Crushed limestone

Contact: Robert G. McKinley
Regional Trail Corporation
PO Box 95
West Newton, PA 15089
724-872-5586
www.atatrail.com
email: yrt@nb.net

Youghiogheny River Trail (South)

This 28-mile segment of the Youghiogheny River Trail (YRT) follows the abandoned Western Maryland Railroad, which was built in 1912. It travels through Ohiopyle State Park, which was named for the Native American word "Ohiopehhle," meaning "white, frothy water."

In 1754, George Washington came down the Yough (pronounced "Yock") hoping to capture Fort Duquesne, but he abandoned all efforts when he saw the great falls at Ohiopyle. Today, Ohiopyle State Park encompasses approximately 19,052 acres of beautiful river scenery and serves as the gateway to the Laurel Mountains. The Youghiogheny River Gorge, famous for its whitewater rafting and kayaking, winds through the park and the YRT (South) follows the river through Ohiopyle State Park from near Connellsville to Confluence.

The Ohiopyle trailhead is located at a restored railroad station serving as an information center with restrooms. Rental outlets for bicycles are located nearby.

To access the trail at milepoint 58 in Connellsville, follow Rt119 South from Pittsburgh to Rt711. Head left on Rt711 to Third Street. Head left on Third and continue to 50-car trailhead parking lot near Riverfront Park. In the town of Connellsville, the YRT follows Third Street. Head north on Third to access the YRT North towards Pittsburgh or access the YRT South towards Cumberland, Md.

To access the trail in Ohiopyle State Park, follow Rt40 southeast from Uniontown to Rt381. Head north on Rt381 to Ohiopyle. Turn right to the Visitor Center, just before crossing the river, and park at the boat take-out/trailhead.

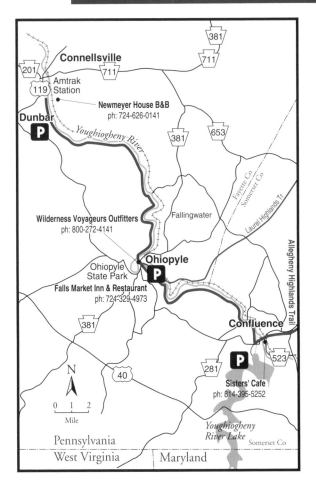

Location:	Fayette and Somerset Counties
Miles:	28
Endpoints:	Confluence to Connellsville
Surface:	Crushed limestone
Contact:	Ohiopyle State Park
	PO Box 105
	Ohiopyle, PA 15470
	724-329-8591
	www.atatrail.org
	www.dcnr.state.pa.us

Index to Trailside Services

Nethercott Inn p. 43

6 Starrucca Creek Rd.
Starrucca, PA 18462
570-727-2211
570-727-3811 (fax)
netheinn@nep.net
www.nethercottinn.com

New Hope Cyclery p. 45

186 Old York Rd.
New Hope, PA 18938
215-862-6888
215-862-3121 (fax)
www.newhopecyclery.com

Pettecote Junction Campground p. 125

400 Beach Rd.
Box 14
Cedar Run, PA 17727
570-353-7183
hometown.aol.com\pettecotejunc

Pine Creek Outfitters, Inc. p. 125

RR#4 Box 130 B
Wellsboro, PA 16901
570-724-3003
pinecrk@clarityconnect.com
www.pinecrk.com

Pocono Whitewater Biking and Skirmish p. 93, 151

HC-2, Box 2245
Jim Thorpe, PA 18229
800-WHITEWATER
rafting@whitewaterrafting.com
www.whitewaterrafting.com

Porches on the Towpath Bed & Breakfast p. 45

20 Fisher's Alley
New Hope, PA 18938
215-862-3277
info@porchesnewhope.com
www.porchesnewhope.com

Quo Vadis Bed & Breakfast p. 9, 133

1501 Liberty St.
Franklin, PA 16323
800-360-6598
www.quovadisbandb.com

R&R Bicycle p. 161

1026 E. Smithfield St.
Boston, PA 15135
412-751-5341
412-751-5357 (fax)
rrbicycle@compuserve.com
www.rrbicycle.com

Rapp's Bicycle Center, Inc. p. 23

179 New Castle Rd.
Butler, PA 16001
724-287-8048
724-283-2453 (fax)

Trenthouse Inn & Country Store   p. 5
2008 Copper Kettle Highway
Rockwood, PA 15557
814-352-7713 / 888-887-5671
www.bbonline.com/pa/trenthouse

Valleyview Farm and Campground   p. 43
RR#1 Box 1348
Waymart, PA 18472
570-448-2268
rvcamp@nep.net

Victorian Loft B&B / Cedarwood Lodge   p. 33
216 S. Front St.
Clearfield, PA 16830
814-765-4805 / 800-798-0456
814-765-9596 (fax)
pdurant@csrlink.net
www.virtualcities.com/pa/victorianloft.htm

Wheelfine Imports   p. 45
639 Brunswick Pike
(on corner of Rt. 518 & Hunter Rd
Lambertville, NJ 08530
609-397-3403
www.wheelfineimports.com

Whistle Stop Bike Shop   p. 61
2 E. Franklin St.
New Freedom, PA 17349
717-227-0737
ehbike@aol.com

Wilderness Voyageurs Outfitters   p. 161,163
PO Box 97
Ohiopyle, PA 15470
724-329-5517 / 800-272-4141
rafting@wilderness-voyageurs.com
www.wilderness-voyageurs.com

Wolfe's General Store/Slate Run Tackle Shop   p. 125
PO Box 1, Route 414
Slate Run, PA 17769
570-753-8551
570-753-8920 (fax)
www.slaterun.com

York Street House Bed and Breakfast   p. 45
42 York Street
Lambertville, NJ 08530
609-397-3007 / 888-398-3199
609-397-3299
Innkeeper@yorkstreethouse.com
www.yorkstreethouse.com

Yorktowne Hotel   p. 61
48 E. Market St.
York, PA 17401
717-848-1111
717-854-7678 (fax)
reservations@yorktowne.com
www.yorktowne.com

About the Rails-to-Trails Conservancy

Established in 1985, RTC is a national nonprofit public charity with more than 8,000 members in Pennsylvania. The mission of Rails-to-Trails Conservancy is to enhance America's communities and countrysides by converting thousands of miles of abandoned rail corridors, and connecting open space, into a nationwide network of public trails. Key objectives RTC undertakes include:

- alerting trail advocates and local governments of upcoming right-of-way abandonments
- assisting public and private agencies in the legalities of trail corridor acquisition
- providing technical assistance to private citizens as well as trail planners, designers, and managers on trail design, development and protection
- publicizing rails-to-trails issues throughout the country.

How to Become an RTC Member

Our efforts are wholly supported by the generous contributions of its members and friends—individuals and families like you. We invite you to join today by filling out the membership form on the opposite side of this page.

Membership/Gift Membership Levels:

Individual Membership	$18
Family Membership	$25
Organization Membership	$50
Business Membership	$100
Advocate Membership	$500
Trailblazer Society Membership	$1000

As a member of RTC, you will receive the following:

- A membership in the national and state organizations
- A subscription to our National Magazine, *Rails-to-Trails*
- A subscription to our newsletter, *Trailblazing Pennsylvania*
- Discounts on books, merchandise and conferences
- Additional benefits for Trailblazer Society members

Most importantly, you help support the Pennsylvania office, giving you a voice in trail development in the Commonwealth and the satisfaction that comes from helping to build a statewide network of beautiful pathways for all of us to enjoy for generations to come.

Rails–to–Trails Conservancy is a nonprofit charitable organization as qualified under Section 501(c)(3) of the Internal Revenue Code.

Contributions are tax deductible to the extent permitted by law.

To obtain a copy of RTC's current financial statement, annual report and state registration, write to RTC at 1100 17th St. NW, Washington, DC 20036, or call 202-331-9696.

Publications

I want ___ copies of the 7th edition *Pennsylvania's Rail-Trails* guidebook. Price includes tax and shipping.

Members	**$16.78**
Non-Members	**$18.90**
Subtotal	$_____

Memberships

My dues enroll me as a member of the Rails-to-Trails Conservancy, Northeast Regional Office.

Individual	**$18**
Family	**$25**
Business	**$100**
Benefactor	**$250**
Advocate	**$500**
Trailblazer	**$1000**
Subtotal	$_____

I want to aid trail efforts in the Commonwealth. I am enclosing an additional gift to the Northeast Regional Office.

	$10
	$25
	$50
	$100
Total	$_____
Payment Type	**Check**
	Visa
	MC

Credit card number _____ - _____ - _____ - _____

Expiration date _____

Signature _____

Make checks to: **Rails to Trails Conservancy**
105 Locust Street
Harrisburg, PA 17101

Name _____
Add. _____
Add. _____
City _____
State _____
Zip _____
Phone _____
Email _____

172